Sales & Marketing Selected Ahadiths

Professor Javed Iqbal Saani

Intellectual Capital Enterprise Limited, London

Copyright © 2017 Prof Javed Iqbal Saani

All rights reserved.

No reproduction of the book in any form such as electronic, photocopying, scanning, recording or otherwise. It also includes storing for retrieval purposes or transmitting through electronic media i.e., email. Prior written permission of the publisher may require doing any of the above under the relevant act that follows the Copyright, Design, and Patent Act 1988.

Authors and the publisher are not responsible for any damage caused by the application/use of the concepts, techniques, instruction, or actions. The authors and publishers refuse any implied warranties or related matters.

Published by Intellectual Capital Enterprise Limited

ICE Kemp House, 152-160 City Road

London, EC1 V2N

Printed in England

CONTENTS

Dedication XI

Acknowledgement XIII

Preface XV

1 INTRODUCTION   1

The product 3
Process 4
Price 5
Place 6
Promotion 6
BUYING gift back 7

2 GENERAL PRINCIPLES   9

INTRODUCTION 9
A-HALAL EARNINGS 12
B- EXPANSION OF SUSTENANCE 14
C-BUYING FOR GIFT 14
D-TRADING IN MARKETPLACE 15
E-DECEPTION 17
F-RAW MATERIAL 19

3 PRODUCT — 21

INTRODUCTION 21
A-SERVICES 23
B-ILLEGAL PRODUCTS.. 25
C-DOUBTFUL PRODUCTS 33

4 PROCESS — 35

INTRODUCTION 35
A-LENIENCY IN BARGAINING 36
B-POSSESSION OF PRODUCT 38
C-CASH / CREDIT SALES 39
D-AL-GHARER TRANSACTIONS 40
E-AL-LIMAS OR MULAMASA (EXAMINATION OF PRODUCT) 41
F-SWEARING 42
G-BARTER 43
H-SELLING OF MIXED DATES (A KIND OF USURY) 50
I-DISCLOSING DEFECTS 52
J- SILK IS UNDESIRABLE TO WEAR BUT ALLOWED TO SELL 53
K-ARAYA 54

5 TERMS OF TRANSACTION — 59

INTRODUCTION 59
A-SELLING AND UN-MILKED ANIMAL 62

B-IMPOSING UNLAWFUL (NOT ALLOWED IN ISLAM) CONDITIONS ... 64

C-THE SALE OF FRUITS BEFORE THEIR BENEFIT IS EVIDENT 65

D- POLLINATED DATES 68

E-THE SALE OF UNHARVESTED CROPS FOR A MEASURED QUANTITY OF FOODSTUFF 69

F-NO FIXED JUDGEMENT 69

G-BROKER 70

H-TIME LIMIT FOR SALE 71

I-JOINT PROPERTY AS A PRODUCT AND THE RIGHT OF PREEMPTION 72

6 PRICE 75

INTRODUCTION 75

A-PAYING IN ADVANCE 76

B-CREDIT PURCHASE 78

7 PLACE 81

INTRODUCTION 81

A- GOING OUT FOR TRADING 83

B- THE SELLING OF THE FOODSTUFF AND ITS STORAGE 84

C-BUYING THE GOODS AWAY FROM THE MARKET 87

8 PROMOTION 89

INTRODUCTION 89

PROMOTION: THE DISLIKE OF RAISING VOICES IN THE MARKET 90

9 VIRTUES OF TRADERS — 93

INTRODUCTION 93
A-VIRTUES OF TRADERS 93
B-MEASUREMENTS 97

10 IMPLICATIONS FOR MANAGERS — 101

GENERAL PRINCIPLES 101
PRODUCT 102
PROCESS 104
TERMS OF TRANSACTIONS 106
PRICE 108
PLACE 108
PROMOTION 110
SHOW FAULT BEFORE SELLING 110
VIRTUES OF TRADE 115
BIBLIOGRAPHY 119
INDEX 123
ABOUT THE AUTHOR 127
OTHER BOOKS BY THE AUTHOR (S) 129
NOTES 131

Abu'd-Darda' (RA) said, "I heard the Messenger of Allah, may Allah bless him and grant him peace, say,

1. 'Allah will make the path to the Garden easy for anyone who travels a path in search of knowledge.
2. Angels spread their wings for the seeker of knowledge out of pleasure for what he is doing.
3. Everyone in the heavens and everyone in the earth asks forgiveness for a man of knowledge, even the fish in the water.
4. The superiority of the man of knowledge to the man of worship is like the superiority of the moon to all the planets.
5. The men of knowledge are the heirs of the Prophets.
6. The Prophets bequeath neither dinar nor dirham; they bequeath knowledge. Whoever takes it has taken an ample part.'"

[Abu Dawud and at-Tirmidhi; Riyadh us Salihin, Hadith 1388, p. 211]

Anas (May Allah be pleased with him) reported:

The Messenger of Allah (ﷺ) said, "He who goes forth in search of knowledge is considered as struggling in the Cause of Allah until he returns."

[At- Tirmidhi].

Dedication

To the entire Ummah who have embraced the message of the prophet (ﷺ) and is sacrificing because they proclaim that Allah is their Rubb, Quran is their book and Muhammad (ﷺ) is their leader.

Acknowledgement

I am obliged to my family who spared me to embark on the project. They also provide valuable information which enriched the contents of this effort. May Allah reward them for their contribution? Ameen!

Preface

One thing is certain in life that is change. The world has been changing since its start though the pace of change is faster today than in the known history. Change brings innovative ideas on the front and the old ones gather dust. However, one can find new facts from the old ideas by blowing away the dust they had gathered over time.

Allah (SWT) sent down Islam for the benefit of humanity till the Last Day; it was complete at its start because the knowledge of Allah is complete. Fundamental needs of humans rarely change. Eating, drinking, and sleeping were there at the time of Adham (Alaiy Slaam), and they are here today. Trade has no exception. People exchange goods and services for their mutual benefit. Sometime with the help of currency and sometimes without it. More specifically, the system was simple in the past but is complex today. However, the nature of the exchange process is the same.

Islam guides its followers how to trade so that both parties should benefit equally and justly. Although the interests of the buyer and seller are inverse there should be an equilibrium so that everyone feels satisfaction. And the experience should be win-win.

Traditional trade changed to marketing which encapsulates the importance of customers and their needs and wants. Islam offers guidelines for both: marketers and customers. The treasure of hadith is full of the 'rules' to take full benefit of the exchange of goods and services. This volume arranges them under five headings: product, process, price, promotion, and place. It might be the only contribution of this work to knowledge. It is only a humble effort towards the subject. There is scholarly work available about it on the 'Net' and on the market. Many well-known journals about Islamic marketing and related subjects are also there. Keen researchers can take benefit of them. This volume is a complement to the existing repository of knowledge on the subject. It consists of 103 ahadith.

The principal source of the work is the Bukhari shareef published by Kazi Publisher and Arabic text has been taken from www.sunnah.com. Nevertheless, we cross checked with the published sources.

Finally, if anything is good in the book, it is with the help and tofeeq of Allah (SWT) and if there are shortcomings (intentional or otherwise) they are mine. I welcome any suggestions to correct them and improve the work in future endeavors.

Professor Javed Iqbal Saani, Ph. D
Manchester
10 April 2017

xviii

1 INTRODUCTION

The trade is a desirable profession because the prophet (ﷺ) himself did it and many eminent companions also. There is a hadith about it that (to the nearest effect) 90% of my ummah's sustenance is in business. (Zakariya, 1979) Marketing is the core of the modern business. Contemporary marketing theorists believe that it is the creation of value for the customer. It involves the exchange of products, services, ideas for the mutual benefit of the parties concerned. The theory evolves from manufacturing centric to consumer orientation. There are certain products which are scary either as a natural resource or as a manufactured product. Their demand is more than production; therefore, the sellers have the upper hand for selling them. He decides their price, distribution channels, and attributes. Sometimes the buyer must place an order for them and wait for delivery. There are a few manufacturers of such products in each geographical area. On the contrary, there are certain products whose manufactures are in abundance and their consumers are also large in number. So, there is cutthroat competition for selling and winning over customers. It created the need and concept of marketing which starts with the identification of customer needs and ends with their satisfaction. Products are made according to the likes and dislikes of customers and sold to them at their convenience. The job of a marketer is to offer attractive products and provide after-sales services. It enables it to develop customer relationships for long-term success.

Modern marketing system consists of four Ps i.e., product, price, place, and promotion. Some variations are also in place such as 5 Ps., 7 Ps etc. This book follows five Ps convention for the sake of simplicity, but the fifth P is Process rather than People. Marketing texts describe them under the broader term marketing mix. A brief review of them is presented here before approaching the treasure of hadith.

It involves the exchange of products, services, and ideas for the mutual benefits of the parties concerned. There are certain products which are scary either as a natural resource or as a manufactured product. Therefore, the sellers have the upper hand for selling them. There are a few manufacturers of such products in each geographical area. On the contrary, there are certain products whose manufactures are in abundance and their consumers are also large in number. Products are made according to the likes and dislikes of customers and sold to them at their convenience. The job of a marketer is to offer attractive products and provide after-sales services. product, price, place, and promotion. Marketing texts describe them under the broader term marketing mix.

THE PRODUCT

The starting point is the product. What is being offered? Emphasis is given to its features, i.e., what are the key components/ingredients of the product being offered for sale which satisfy the users. The product is broad term, which also includes services and the way they are given to the clients. Marketing theory rarely mentions the ethical part of the product i.e., which products should be sold/traded and which should not. Also, there is little agreement about what is legal at the international level. Some products might be legal in some parts of the world, but they are illegal elsewhere. For example, production and trade of drugs and wine.

Islamic teachings classify products based on permissible and non-permissible for the betterment of the society at large. Therefore, this collection of ahadiths informs us about the products allowed to trade or manufacture. These are placed in a separate section.

PROCESS

Sometimes a product is legal for trade or consumption but its way of trade is not permissible. We call it 'process'. For instance, inferior quality products cannot be traded with superior quality products of the same category e.g., dates. It is recommended that the former should be sold for money and the superior quality products may be bought. It is because the inferiority of some products cannot be decided easily or not at all. Thus, it is simple to sell inferior products and buy superior products. It also protects the rights of those who offer inferior products; the owner of superior products can ask for or decide the exchange rate as he likes. The matter has been placed in a separate section and is called 'process.'

A related issue was the terms of trade, which looks like the process but they are different, therefore, placed in a separate chapter for the sake of simplicity and to make them understandable.

PRICE

Price is decided by the owner of the product in the first instance. However, it is settled with the mutual consent of the parties concerned. Agreement at a certain price is a compulsory condition of a bargain.[1] The price is valid until the parties separate in cash or face-to-face transaction. E-commerce and online transactions are also part of it since the websites being the seller and the buyer uses it as a tool for the bargain.

Price also includes some services such as delivery or after-sales services as part of the package. It should fulfill the conditions included in the purchase. Many service organizations sell their services for a monthly premium or one-off payment such as British Gas sells boiler care package. The

---

[1] Tofatul Qari, V 5, p.129.

seller must do it for the specified period at the agreed upon price.

PLACE

The place is the third partner of the marketing mix. The true value of the product is always decided in the market. The market does not necessarily mean a geographical area because online trade is free from such boundaries. If someone wants to know the price of a used car in the UK, he can consult Auto Trader (or its website). Islamic teachings emphasize the role of markets. The prophet (ﷺ) recommended that people bring the goods to the markets (details are placed in the section on the place). It was especially relevant at the time when the prophet (the prophet(when people used to buy stuff from the caravans coming from other countries but did not enter the city of Makkah i.e., the marketplace. The practice was prohibited because the seller did not know the market value of their goods.

PROMOTION

The literature I have consulted offers little about promotion. One hadith mentioned raising voices in the market. The prophet (ﷺ) did not like it.

When caravans used to arrive in the city, the seller was beating drums to announce their arrival. It was the information for the buyers. It is assumed that interested merchants and consumers would approach the caravan. People, in general, keep informing themselves about the arrival of caravans to do some trade. History shows that trade caravans were frequent which were arriving from Syria and Yemen. Yemeni cloths were popular and expensive. Egyptian products were also well known. Hazrat Abdur Rehman bin Ouff's (RA) caravans were famous in Madinah.

Given this brief, let us move towards the subject.

BUYING GIFT BACK

"On the way I conversed with the Messenger of God, and he said to me: "Wilt thou sell me this camel of thine?" I said: "I will give him to thee." "Nay," he said, "but sell him to me." Jabir knew from the tone of the Prophet's voice that he was expected to bargain. "I asked him," said Jabir, "to name me a price and he said: 'I will take him for a dirham.' 'Not so,' I said, 'for then wouldst thou be giving me too little.' 'For two dirhems,' he said. 'Nay,' said I, and he went on raising his price until he reached forty.

dirhems, that is, an ounce of gold, to which I agreed.

Then he said: 'Art thou yet married, Jabir?' And when I said that I was, he said: 'An already married woman or a virgin?' 'One already married,' I said 'Why not a girl,' he said, 'that thou might's play with her and she with thee?' 'O Messenger of God,' I said, 'my father was struck down on the day of Uhud and left me with his seven daughters, so I married a motherly woman who would gather them round her and comb their hair and look after their wants.' He agreed that I had made an excellent choice; and then he said that when we reached Sirar, which was only about three miles from Medina, he would sacrifice camels and spend the day there, and she would have news of our home-coming and would set about shaking the dust from her cushions. 'We have no cushions,' I said. 'They will come,' he said. 'So, when thou returnest, do what is to be done.'

"The morning after we returned, I took my camel and knelt him outside the Prophet's door. The Prophet came out and told me to leave the camel and pray two prayer cycles in the Mosque, which I did. Then he bade Bilal weigh me out an ounce of gold, and he gave me a little more than what tipped the scales. I took it and turned to go, but the Prophet called me back. 'Take thy camel,' he said, 'he is thine, and keep the price thou wast paid for him.'[2]

---

[2] Lings, p. 209.

2 GENERAL PRINCIPLES

INTRODUCTION

The chapter includes the common themes which apply to the discipline of marketing. Since the book divides the subject into five categories, the topics of the chapter are useful for all of them. It consists of six subheadings and fourteen ahadith.

The starting point is the means of one's earnings; Islam emphasizes the legal sources of making a livelihood. Therefore, trading halal products have been differentiated from the haram. For example, wine, pigs and dogs are harams to drink and eat, consequently, their trade is also haram. The first hadith reiterates the importance of earning through work [business or job]. The prophet (ﷺ) refers to the practice of Daud Alyheslaam. The prophet (ﷺ) of Islam also worked for someone and did business as well prior to the announcement of prophethood. After which he did not have time out of the work of dawah to do anything else. Allah (SWT) the exalted, commanded him to do the work of dawah and the sustenance would be provided to him.

> And enjoy upon thy people worship and be constant there. We ask not of thee a provision: We provided for thee. And the sequel is for righteousness. [Surah Taha: 132]

Another example of Abu Bakr (RA) was described; he wanted to continue his profession of trade when he became the caliph; Umer (RA) suggested an alternative which Abu Bakr accepted. Finally, the warning was given about a time when people would not care about their source of earnings.

Secondly, making more money through working seems more natural. But spending a lot of time on earning limits the ability to spare time for looking after relatives or for the cause of social activities. Consequently, busy businesspersons cannot participate in funeral prayers, or are unable to visit sick people. It is recommended that an increase in sustenance is not associated with the amount of income, but it appears out of the social relations one has with his relatives.

The idea has been further expanded through the exchange of gifts. Sometimes the gifts are more useful when the recipient is in dire need of food or necessities. The hadith mentioned here describes that the prophet (ﷺ) bought a camel from father and presented to his son. The family benefited twice from a sole source/transaction.

The next topic deals with the place of business transactions. A chapter has been given for the subject. Emphasis is given about the importance of the marketplace where both buyer and seller are aware of the price. They can exchange goods willingly and at the right rates. Both parties receive their fair share out of the bargain they are involved in. It safeguards the rights of both individuals/parties. The purpose is to make purchasing experience a win-win game.

The topic is augmented with one of the possibilities i.e., deception. The attempt of deception either implicitly or explicitly is prohibited. For instance, swearing strengthens the argument of the seller but it was an undesirable practice. So, the traders were suggested to do some charitable work to offset the impacts of it though the sellers were not misrepresenting their products.

Finally, a natural product was protected, i.e., grass was not allowed to cut except for using it as raw material for goldsmiths or for covering graves. The grass was known as Al-Idhkhir. It draws the ethical line for the business community.

A-HALAL EARNINGS

حَدَّثَنَا إِبْرَاهِيمُ بْنُ مُوسَى، أَخْبَرَنَا عِيسَى، عَنْ ثَوْرٍ، عَنْ خَالِدِ بْنِ مَعْدَانَ، عَنِ الْمِقْدَامِ ـ رضى الله عنه ـ عَنْ رَسُولِ اللَّهِ صلى الله عليه وسلم قَالَ " مَا أَكَلَ أَحَدٌ طَعَامًا قَطُّ خَيْرًا مِنْ أَنْ يَأْكُلَ مِنْ عَمَلِ يَدِهِ، وَإِنَّ نَبِيَّ اللَّهِ دَاوُدَ ـ عَلَيْهِ السَّلاَمُ ـ كَانَ يَأْكُلُ مِنْ عَمَلِ يَدِهِ ".

1-Narrated Al-Miqdam:

Prophet (ﷺ) said, "Nobody has ever eaten a better meal than that which one has earned by working with one's own hands. The Prophet (ﷺ) of Allah, David used to eat from the earnings of his manual labor." [Al-Bukhari, Book 34, Hadith 25]

حَدَّثَنَا إِسْمَاعِيلُ بْنُ عَبْدِ اللَّهِ، قَالَ حَدَّثَنِي ابْنُ وَهْبٍ، عَنْ يُونُسَ، عَنِ ابْنِ شِهَابٍ، قَالَ حَدَّثَنِي عُرْوَةُ بْنُ الزُّبَيْرِ، أَنَّ عَائِشَةَ ـ رضى الله عنها ـ قَالَتْ لَمَّا اسْتُخْلِفَ أَبُو بَكْرٍ الصِّدِّيقُ قَالَ لَقَدْ عَلِمَ قَوْمِي أَنَّ حِرْفَتِي لَمْ تَكُنْ تَعْجِزُ عَنْ

مَئُونَةَ أَهْلِي، وَشُغِلْتُ بِأَمْرِ الْمُسْلِمِينَ، فَسَيَأْكُلُ آلُ أَبِي بَكْرٍ مِنْ هَذَا الْمَالِ وَيَحْتَرِفُ لِلْمُسْلِمِينَ فِيهِ.

2-Narrated `Aisha:

When Abu Bakr As-Siddiq was chosen as Caliph, he said, "My people know that my profession was not incapable of providing substance to my family. And as I will be busy serving the Muslim nation, my family will eat from the National Treasury of Muslims, and I will practice the profession of serving the Muslims." [Al-Bukhari, Book 34, Hadith 23]

حَدَّثَنَا يَحْيَى بْنُ مُوسَى، حَدَّثَنَا عَبْدُ الرَّزَّاقِ، أَخْبَرَنَا مَعْمَرٌ، عَنْ هَمَّامِ بْنِ مُنَبِّهٍ، حَدَّثَنَا أَبُو هُرَيْرَةَ، عَنْ رَسُولِ اللَّهِ صلى الله عليه وسلم " أَنَّ دَاوُدَ ـ عَلَيْهِ السَّلاَمُ ـ كَانَ لاَ يَأْكُلُ إِلاَّ مِنْ عَمَلِ يَدِهِ ".

3-Narrated Abu Huraira:

Allah's Messenger (ﷺ) said, "The Prophet David (AS) used not to eat except <u>the earnings of his manual labor.</u>" [Al-Bukhari, Book 34, Hadith 26]

حَدَّثَنَا آدَمُ، حَدَّثَنَا ابْنُ أَبِي ذِئْبٍ، حَدَّثَنَا سَعِيدٌ الْمَقْبُرِيُّ، عَنْ أَبِي هُرَيْرَةَ ـ رضى الله عنه ـ عَنِ النَّبِيِّ صلى الله عليه وسلم قَالَ " يَأْتِي عَلَى النَّاسِ زَمَانٌ، لاَ يُبَالِي الْمَرْءُ مَا أَخَذَ مِنْهُ أَمِنَ الْحَلاَلِ أَمْ مِنَ الْحَرَامِ ".

4-Narrated Abu Huraira:

The Prophet (ﷺ) said, "A time will come when one will not care how one gains one's money, legally or illegally." [Al-Bukhari Book 34, Hadith 13]

B- EXPANSION OF SUSTENANCE

حَدَّثَنَا مُحَمَّدُ بْنُ أَبِي يَعْقُوبَ الْكِرْمَانِيُّ، حَدَّثَنَا حَسَّانُ، حَدَّثَنَا يُونُسُ، حَدَّثَنَا مُحَمَّدٌ، عَنْ أَنَسِ بْنِ مَالِكٍ ـ رضى الله عنه ـ قَالَ سَمِعْتُ رَسُولَ اللَّهِ صلى الله عليه وسلم يَقُولُ " مَنْ سَرَّهُ أَنْ يُبْسَطَ لَهُ رِزْقُهُ أَوْ يُنْسَأَ لَهُ فِي أَثَرِهِ فَلْيَصِلْ رَحِمَهُ ".

5-Narrated Anas bin Malik:

I heard Allah's Messenger (ﷺ) saying, "whoever desires an expansion in his sustenance and age, should keep good relations with his Kith and kin." [Al-Bukhari, Book 34, Hadith 20]

C-BUYING FOR GIFT

وَقَالَ الْحُمَيْدِيُّ حَدَّثَنَا سُفْيَانُ، حَدَّثَنَا عَمْرٌو، عَنِ ابْنِ عُمَرَ ـ رضى الله عنهما ـ قَالَ كُنَّا مَعَ النَّبِيِّ صلى الله عليه وسلم فِي سَفَرٍ فَكُنْتُ عَلَى بَكْرٍ صَعْبٍ لِعُمَرَ، فَكَانَ يَغْلِبُنِي فَيَتَقَدَّمُ أَمَامَ الْقَوْمِ، فَيَزْجُرُهُ عُمَرُ وَيَرُدُّهُ، ثُمَّ يَتَقَدَّمُ فَيَزْجُرُهُ عُمَرُ وَيَرُدُّهُ فَقَالَ النَّبِيُّ صلى الله عليه وسلم لِعُمَرَ " بِعْنِيهِ ". قَالَ هُوَ لَكَ يَا رَسُولَ اللَّهِ. قَالَ " بِعْنِيهِ ". فَبَاعَهُ مِنْ رَسُولِ اللَّهِ صلى الله عليه وسلم فَقَالَ النَّبِيُّ صلى الله عليه وسلم " هُوَ لَكَ يَا عَبْدَ اللَّهِ بْنَ عُمَرَ تَصْنَعُ بِهِ مَا شِئْتَ ".

6-Narrated Ibn 'Umar (RA):

We were going with the Prophet (ﷺ) on a journey and I was riding an unmanageable camel belonging to 'Umar (RA), and I could not bring it under my control. So, it used to go ahead of the party and 'Umar would check it and force it to retreat, and again it went ahead and again 'Umar forced it to retreat. The Prophet (ﷺ) asked 'Umar to sell that camel to him. 'Umar replied, "It is for you O Allah's Messenger!" Allah's Messenger (ﷺ) told 'Umar to sell that camel to him (not to give it as a gift). So, 'Umar sold it to Allah's Messenger (ﷺ). Then the Prophet (ﷺ) said to 'Abdullah bin 'Umar "This camel is for you O 'Abdullah (as a present) and you could do with it whatever you like." [Al-Bukhari, Book 34, Hadith 68]

D-TRADING IN MARKETPLACE

حَدَّثَنَا مُحَمَّدُ بْنُ بَشَّارٍ، حَدَّثَنَا عَبْدُ الْوَهَّابِ، حَدَّثَنَا عُبَيْدُ اللَّهِ، عَنْ سَعِيدِ بْنِ أَبِي سَعِيدٍ، عَنْ أَبِي هُرَيْرَةَ ـ رضى الله عنه ـ قَالَ نَهَى النَّبِيُّ صلى الله عليه وسلم عَنِ التَّلَقِّي، وَأَنْ يَبِيعَ حَاضِرٌ لِبَادٍ‏.‏

7-Narrated Abu Huraira:

The Prophet (ﷺ) forbade the meeting (of caravans) on the way and the selling of goods by an inhabitant of the town on behalf of a desert dweller. [Al-Bukhari, Book 34, Hadith 113]

حَدَّثَنَا مُسَدَّدٌ، حَدَّثَنَا يَزِيدُ بْنُ زُرَيْعٍ، قَالَ حَدَّثَنِي التَّيْمِيُّ، عَنْ أَبِي عُثْمَانَ، عَنْ عَبْدِ اللَّهِ ـ رضى الله عنه ـ قَالَ مَنِ اشْتَرَى مُحَفَّلَةً فَلْيَرُدَّ مَعَهَا صَاعًا. قَالَ وَنَهَى النَّبِيُّ صلى الله عليه وسلم عَنْ تَلَقِّي الْبُيُوعِ.

8-Narrated `Abdullah:

Whoever buys an animal which has been kept un-milked for a long time, could return it, but has to pay a Sa of dates along with it. And the Prophet (ﷺ) forbade meeting the owners of goods on the way away from the market. [Al-Bukhari, Book 34, Hadith 115]

حَدَّثَنَا عَبْدُ اللَّهِ بْنُ يُوسُفَ، أَخْبَرَنَا مَالِكٌ، عَنْ نَافِعٍ، عَنْ عَبْدِ اللَّهِ بْنِ عُمَرَ ـ رضى الله عنهما ـ أَنَّ رَسُولَ اللَّهِ صلى الله عليه وسلم قَالَ " لاَ يَبِيعُ بَعْضُكُمْ عَلَى بَيْعِ بَعْضٍ، وَلاَ تَلَقَّوُا السِّلَعَ حَتَّى يُهْبَطَ بِهَا إِلَى السُّوقِ ".

9-Narrated `Abdullah bin `Umar:

Allah's Messenger (ﷺ) said, "You should not try to cancel the purchases of one another (to get a benefit thereof), and do not go ahead to meet the caravan (for buying the goods) (but wait) till it reaches the market." [Al-Bukhari, Book 34, Hadith 116]

E-DECEPTION

حَدَّثَنَا يَحْيَى بْنُ يَحْيَى، وَيَحْيَى بْنُ أَيُّوبَ، وَقُتَيْبَةُ، وَابْنُ حُجْرٍ قَالَ يَحْيَى بْنُ يَحْيَى أَخْبَرَنَا وَقَالَ الآخَرُونَ، حَدَّثَنَا إِسْمَاعِيلُ بْنُ جَعْفَرٍ، عَنْ عَبْدِ اللَّهِ بْنِ دِينَارٍ، أَنَّهُ سَمِعَ ابْنَ، عُمَرَ يَقُولُ ذَكَرَ رَجُلٌ لِرَسُولِ اللَّهِ صلى الله عليه وسلم أَنَّهُ يُخْدَعُ فِي الْبُيُوعِ فَقَالَ رَسُولُ اللَّهِ صلى الله عليه وسلم " مَنْ بَايَعْتَ فَقُلْ لاَ خِلاَبَةَ ". فَكَانَ إِذَا بَايَعَ يَقُولُ لاَ خِيَابَةَ.

10-Abdullah b. Dinar narrated:

that he heard Ibn 'Umar (Allah be pleased with them) saying: A man mentioned to the Messenger of Allah (ﷺ) that he was deceived in a business transaction, whereupon Allah's Messenger (ﷺ) said:

When you enter into a transaction, say: There should be no attempt to <u>deceive</u>. [Sahih Muslim, Book 21, Hadith 59]

حَدَّثَنَا مُسَدَّدٌ، حَدَّثَنَا أَبُو مُعَاوِيَةَ، عَنِ الأَعْمَشِ، عَنْ أَبِي وَائِلٍ، عَنْ قَيْسِ بْنِ أَبِي غَرَزَةَ، قَالَ كُنَّا فِي عَهْدِ رَسُولِ اللَّهِ صلى الله عليه وسلم نُسَمَّى السَّمَاسِرَةَ فَمَرَّ بِنَا رَسُولُ اللَّهِ صلى الله عليه وسلم فَسَمَّانَا بِاسْمٍ هُوَ أَحْسَنُ مِنْهُ فَقَالَ " يَا مَعْشَرَ التُّجَّارِ إِنَّ الْبَيْعَ يَحْضُرُهُ اللَّغْوُ وَالْحَلِفُ فَشُوبُوهُ بِالصَّدَقَةِ ".

11-Narrated Qays ibn Abu Gharazah:

In the time of the Messenger of Allah (ﷺ) we used to be called brokers, but the Prophet (ﷺ) came upon us one day, and called us by a better name than that, saying: O company of merchants, unprofitable speech and swearing takes place in business dealings, so mix it with <u>Sadaqah</u> (alms). [Sunan Abi Dawud, Book 23, Hadith 1]

The purpose is to tell sellers to avoid swearing to sell their products. Sometimes it is considered as a tool for selling those products that may not be bought in normal circumstances. The buyer may feel more confident when someone swears. Under such circumstances which may occur occasionally, but Allah (SWT) may not like it. Therefore, the displeasure of Allah (SWT) may be removed with added sadaqa.

حَدَّثَنَا أَحْمَدُ بْنُ عَمْرِو بْنِ السَّرْحِ، حَدَّثَنَا ابْنُ وَهْبٍ، ح وَحَدَّثَنَا أَحْمَدُ بْنُ صَالِحٍ، حَدَّثَنَا عَنْبَسَةُ، عَنْ يُونُسَ، عَنِ ابْنِ شِهَابٍ، قَالَ قَالَ ابْنُ الْمُسَيَّبِ إِنَّ أَبَا هُرَيْرَةَ قَالَ سَمِعْتُ رَسُولَ اللَّهِ صلى الله عليه وسلم يَقُولُ " الْحَلِفُ مَنْفَقَةٌ لِلسِّلْعَةِ مَمْحَقَةٌ لِلْبَرَكَةِ". قَالَ ابْنُ السَّرْحِ " لِلْكَسْبِ ". وَقَالَ عَنْ سَعِيدِ بْنِ الْمُسَيَّبِ عَنْ أَبِي هُرَيْرَةَ عَنِ النَّبِيِّ صلى الله عليه وسلم .

12-Narrated Abu Hurairah:

I heard Messenger of Allah (ﷺ) say: <u>Swearing</u> produces a ready sale for a commodity but blots out the blessing. The narrator Ibn al-Sarh said: "for earning". He also narrated this tradition from Sa'id b. al-Musayyab on the authority of Abu Hurairah from the Prophet (ﷺ). [Sunan Abi Dawud, Book 23, Hadith 10]

حَدَّثَنَا عَبْدُ اللَّهِ بْنُ يُوسُفَ، أَخْبَرَنَا مَالِكٌ، عَنْ عَبْدِ اللَّهِ بْنِ دِينَارٍ، عَنْ عَبْدِ اللَّهِ بْنِ عُمَرَ ـ رضى الله عنهما ـ أَنَّ رَجُلاً، ذَكَرَ لِلنَّبِيِّ صلى الله عليه وسلم أَنَّهُ يُخْدَعُ فِي الْبُيُوعِ، فَقَالَ " إِذَا بَايَعْتَ فَقُلْ لاَ خِلاَبَةَ ".

13- Narrated `Abdullah bin `Umar:

A person came to the Prophet (ﷺ) and told him that he was always betrayed in purchasing. The Prophet (ﷺ) told him to say at the time of buying, "<u>No cheating</u>." [Al-Bukhari, Book 34, Hadith 70]

F-RAW MATERIAL

حَدَّثَنَا إِسْحَاقُ، حَدَّثَنَا خَالِدُ بْنُ عَبْدِ اللَّهِ، عَنْ خَالِدٍ، عَنْ عِكْرِمَةَ، عَنِ ابْنِ عَبَّاسٍ ـ رضى الله عنهما ـ أَنَّ رَسُولَ اللَّهِ صلى الله عليه وسلم قَالَ " إِنَّ اللَّهَ حَرَّمَ مَكَّةَ، وَلَمْ تَحِلَّ لأَحَدٍ قَبْلِي، وَلاَ لأَحَدٍ بَعْدِي، وَإِنَّمَا حَلَّتْ لِي سَاعَةً مِنْ نَهَارٍ، وَلاَ يُخْتَلَى خَلاَهَا، وَلاَ يُعْضَدُ شَجَرُهَا، وَلاَ يُنَفَّرُ صَيْدُهَا وَلاَ يُلْتَقَطُ لُقَطَتُهَا إِلاَّ لِمُعَرِّفٍ ". وَقَالَ عَبَّاسُ بْنُ عَبْدِ الْمُطَّلِبِ إِلاَّ الإِذْخِرَ لِصَاغَتِنَا وَلِسُقُفِ بُيُوتِنَا. فَقَالَ " إِلاَّ الإِذْخِرَ ". فَقَالَ عِكْرِمَةُ هَلْ تَدْرِي مَا يُنَفَّرُ صَيْدُهَا هُوَ أَنْ تُنَحِّيَهُ مِنَ الظِّلِّ، وَتَنْزِلَ مَكَانَهُ. قَالَ عَبْدُ الْوَهَّابِ عَنْ خَالِدٍ لِصَاغَتِنَا وَقُبُورِنَا.

14- Narrated Ibn `Abbas:

Allah's Messenger (ﷺ) said, "Allah made Mecca a sanctuary and it was neither permitted for anyone before nor will it be permitted for anyone after me (to fight in it). And fighting in it was made legal for me for a few hours of a day only. None is allowed to uproot its thorny shrubs or to cut down its trees or to chase its game or to pick up its Luqta (fallen things) except by a person who would announce it publicly." `Abba's bin `Abdul-Muttalib requested the Prophet, "Except Al-Idhkhir, for our goldsmiths and for the roofs of our houses." The Prophet (ﷺ) said, "Except Al-Idhkhir." `Ikrima said, "Do you know what is meant by chasing its game? It is to drive it out of the shade and sit in its place." Khalid said, "(`Abbas said: Al-Idhkhir) for our goldsmiths and our graves." [Al-Bukhari, Book 34, Hadith 43]

The purpose is to save the greenery that grows on its own in the holy land; however, "Al-Idhkhir" (a kind of grass) was exempted because goldsmiths were using it as raw material.

3 PRODUCT

INTRODUCTION

A product is the physical artifact, or services gave to make money. Islamic teaching allows certain products for sale, but their use is not permissible. Those not allowed are not beneficial for human consumption. For instance, wine. The holy book says to the nearest effect that there are some benefits for consuming it but there are more harms. Therefore, it is prohibited. The Creator knows the merits and demerits of a product better.

The topic of this chapter is to know what is permissible and what is not. However, the list of prohibited products is not exhaustive rather than it is only indicative. Since the list of halal products is long, they were not mentioned. We have included some of the haram products in the following paragraphs as a sample rather than a complete catalog. Interested readers can approach Islamic scholars to have such a list.

Some products are halal for a female such as gold and silk while male folk cannot wear them. Nevertheless, their trade is halal. Similarly, some services are allowed, and some are not such as prostitution. In addition, the price of a dog (trade of dogs), tattoos, interest, and earnings of soothsayer are out of the halal circle.

The chapter consists of three sections: the first deals with services, the second haram products, and the final investigates doubtful products. And it has sixteen ahadith. It implies all products are halal except those declared as haram. The chapter presents only a sample of the haram catalog.

Three types of services are described here; the prophet employed the services of a carpenter, a barber, and a copper. Watering trees, plucking dates, and guides were also hired.

Illegal products include the hides of dead animals before tanning, the fat of the dead animal, selling [and making] of the pictures, alcoholic drinks, sale of a free man, sale of dead animals and idols, price of a dog, tattoos, prostitution, interest and soothsayer, unborn baby of animals, selling of silver for gold on delayed payment, and any doubtful product.

A-SERVICES

Employment of a carpenter

حَدَّثَنَا قُتَيْبَةُ بْنُ سَعِيدٍ، حَدَّثَنَا عَبْدُ الْعَزِيزِ، عَنْ أَبِي حَازِمٍ، قَالَ أَتَى رِجَالٌ إِلَى سَهْلِ بْنِ سَعْدٍ يَسْأَلُونَهُ عَنِ الْمِنْبَرِ، فَقَالَ بَعَثَ رَسُولُ اللَّهِ صلى الله عليه وسلم إِلَى فُلاَنَةَ ـ امْرَأَةٍ قَدْ سَمَّاهَا سَهْلٌ ـ " أَنْ مُرِي غُلاَمَكِ النَّجَّارَ، يَعْمَلْ لِي أَعْوَادًا أَجْلِسُ عَلَيْهِنَّ إِذَا كَلَّمْتُ النَّاسَ ". فَأَمَرَتْهُ يَعْمَلُهَا مِنْ طَرْفَاءِ الْغَابَةِ ثُمَّ جَاءَ بِهَا، فَأَرْسَلَتْ إِلَى رَسُولِ اللَّهِ صلى الله عليه وسلم بِهَا، فَأَمَرَ بِهَا فَوُضِعَتْ، فَجَلَسَ عَلَيْهِ.

1-Narrated Abu Hazim:

Some men came to Sahl bin Sa`d to ask him about the pulpit. He replied, "Allah's Messenger (ﷺ) sent for a woman (Sahl named her) (this message): <u>'Order your slave carpenter to make pieces of wood (i.e. a pulpit) for me so that I may sit on it while addressing the people.'</u> So, she ordered him to make it from the tamarisk of the forest. He brought it to her, and she sent it to Allah's Messenger (ﷺ). Allah's Messenger (ﷺ) ordered it to be placed in the mosque: so, it was put, and he sat on it. [Al-Bukhari, Book 34, Hadith 47/2094]

Al-Hajjam (i.e., The one who practices cupping)

حَدَّثَنَا عَبْدُ اللَّهِ بْنُ يُوسُفَ، أَخْبَرَنَا مَالِكٌ، عَنْ حُمَيْدٍ، عَنْ أَنَسِ بْنِ مَالِكٍ ـ رضى الله عنه ـ قَالَ حَجَمَ أَبُو طَيْبَةَ رَسُولَ اللَّهِ صلى الله عليه وسلم فَأَمَرَ لَهُ بِصَاعٍ مِنْ تَمْرٍ، وَأَمَرَ أَهْلَهُ أَنْ يُخَفِّفُوا مِنْ خَرَاجِهِ.

2-Narrated Anas bin Malik:

Abu Taiba cupped Allah's Messenger (ﷺ) so he ordered that he be paid one Sa of dates and ordered his masters to reduce his tax (as he was a slave and had to pay a tax to them). [Al-Bukhari, Book 34, Hadith 55]

حَدَّثَنَا مُسَدَّدٌ، حَدَّثَنَا خَالِدٌ، ـ هُوَ ابْنُ عَبْدِ اللَّهِ ـ حَدَّثَنَا خَالِدٌ، عَنْ عِكْرِمَةَ، عَنِ ابْنِ عَبَّاسٍ ـ رضى الله عنهما ـ قَالَ احْتَجَمَ النَّبِيُّ صلى الله عليه وسلم وَأَعْطَى الَّذِي حَجَمَهُ، وَلَوْ كَانَ حَرَامًا لَمْ يُعْطِهِ.

Copping

3-Narrated Ibn `Abbas:

Once the Prophet (ﷺ) got his blood out (medically) and paid that person who had done it. If it had been illegal, the Prophet (ﷺ) would not have paid him. [Al-Bukhari, Book 34, Hadith 56]

Considering both ahadith the writer of Iman Bari concludes that the profession of cupping is permissible. Where its undesirableness has been expressed it means the profession involves indecent activities. (Allah knows better)

B-ILLEGAL PRODUCTS

They are described under nine sub-headings to make them easy to understand.

The hides of dead animals before tanning

حَدَّثَنَا زُهَيْرُ بْنُ حَرْبٍ، حَدَّثَنَا يَعْقُوبُ بْنُ إِبْرَاهِيمَ، حَدَّثَنَا أَبِي، عَنْ صَالِحٍ، قَالَ حَدَّثَنِي ابْنُ شِهَابٍ، أَنَّ عُبَيْدَ اللَّهِ بْنَ عَبْدِ اللَّهِ، أَخْبَرَهُ أَنَّ عَبْدَ اللَّهِ بْنَ عَبَّاسٍ ـ رضى الله عنهما ـ أَخْبَرَهُ أَنَّ رَسُولَ اللَّهِ صلى الله عليه وسلم مَرَّ بِشَاةٍ مَيِّتَةٍ فَقَالَ " هَلاَّ اسْتَمْتَعْتُمْ بِإِهَابِهَا ". قَالُوا إِنَّهَا مَيِّتَةٌ. قَالَ " إِنَّمَا حَرُمَ أَكْلُهَا ".

4-Narrated `Abdullah bin `Abbas:

Once Allah's Messenger (ﷺ) passed by a dead sheep and said to the people, "<u>Wouldn't you benefit by its skin?</u>" The people replied that it was dead. The Prophet (ﷺ) said, "But eating only is illegal." [Al-Bukhari, Book 34, Hadith 168]

The fat of the dead animal

حَدَّثَنَا الْحُمَيْدِيُّ، حَدَّثَنَا سُفْيَانُ، حَدَّثَنَا عَمْرُو بْنُ دِينَارٍ، قَالَ أَخْبَرَنِي طَاوُسٌ، أَنَّهُ سَمِعَ ابْنَ عَبَّاسٍ ـ رضى الله عنهما ـ يَقُولُ بَلَغَ عُمَرَ أَنَّ فُلاَنًا بَاعَ خَمْرًا فَقَالَ قَاتَلَ اللَّهُ فُلاَنًا، أَلَمْ يَعْلَمْ أَنَّ رَسُولَ اللَّهِ صلى الله عليه وسلم قَالَ " قَاتَلَ

اللَّهُ الْيَهُودَ، حُرِّمَتْ عَلَيْهِمُ الشُّحُومُ فَجَمَلُوهَا فَبَاعُوهَا ".

5-Narrated Ibn `Abbas:

Once `Umar was informed that a certain man sold alcohol. `Umar said, "May Allah curse him! Doesn't he know that Allah's Messenger (ﷺ) said, 'May Allah curse the Jews, for Allah, had forbidden them to eat the fat of animals but they melted it and sold it." [Al-Bukhari, Book 34, Hadith 170]

The selling of the pictures

حَدَّثَنَا عَبْدُ اللَّهِ بْنُ عَبْدِ الْوَهَّابِ، حَدَّثَنَا يَزِيدُ بْنُ زُرَيْعٍ، أَخْبَرَنَا عَوْفٌ، عَنْ سَعِيدِ بْنِ أَبِي الْحَسَنِ، قَالَ كُنْتُ عِنْدَ ابْنِ عَبَّاسٍ ـ رضى الله عنهما ـ إِذْ أَتَاهُ رَجُلٌ فَقَالَ يَا أَبَا عَبَّاسٍ إِنِّي إِنْسَانٌ، إِنَّمَا مَعِيشَتِي مِنْ صَنْعَةِ يَدِي، وَإِنِّي أَصْنَعُ هَذِهِ التَّصَاوِيرَ. فَقَالَ ابْنُ عَبَّاسٍ لاَ أُحَدِّثُكَ إِلاَّ مَا سَمِعْتُ رَسُولَ اللَّهِ صلى الله عليه وسلم يَقُولُ سَمِعْتُهُ يَقُولُ " مَنْ صَوَّرَ صُورَةً فَإِنَّ اللَّهَ مُعَذِّبُهُ، حَتَّى يَنْفُخَ فِيهَا الرُّوحَ، وَلَيْسَ بِنَافِخٍ فِيهَا أَبَدًا ". فَرَبَا الرَّجُلُ رَبْوَةً شَدِيدَةً وَاصْفَرَّ وَجْهُهُ. فَقَالَ وَيْحَكَ إِنْ أَبَيْتَ إِلاَّ أَنْ تَصْنَعَ، فَعَلَيْكَ بِهَذَا الشَّجَرِ، كُلِّ شَيْءٍ لَيْسَ فِيهِ رُوحٌ. قَالَ أَبُو عَبْدِ اللَّهِ سَمِعَ سَعِيدُ بْنُ أَبِي عَرُوبَةَ مِنَ النَّضْرِ بْنِ أَنَسٍ هَذَا الْوَاحِدَ.

6-Narrated Sa`id bin Abu Al-Hasan:

While I was with Ibn `Abbas a man came, and said, "O father of `Abbas! My sustenance is from my manual profession, and I make these pictures." Ibn `Abbas said, "I will tell you only what I heard from Allah's Messenger (ﷺ). I heard him saying, 'Whoever takes a picture will be punished by Allah till he puts life in it, and he will never be able to put life in it.' " Hearing this, that man heaved a sigh and his face turned pale. Ibn `Abbas said to him, "What a pity! If you insist on taking pictures, I advise you to make pictures of trees and any other unanimated objects." [Al-Bukhari, Book 34, Hadith 172]

Trade in alcoholic drinks is illegal.

حَدَّثَنَا مُسْلِمٌ، حَدَّثَنَا شُعْبَةُ، عَنِ الأَعْمَشِ، عَنْ أَبِي الضُّحَى، عَنْ مَسْرُوقٍ، عَنْ عَائِشَةَ ـ رضى الله عنها ـ لَمَّا نَزَلَتْ آيَاتُ سُورَةِ الْبَقَرَةِ عَنْ آخِرِهَا خَرَجَ النَّبِيُّ صلى الله عليه وسلم فَقَالَ " حُرِّمَتِ التِّجَارَةُ فِي الْخَمْرِ ".

7-Narrated `Aisha:

When the last verses of Surat-al-Baqarah were revealed, the Prophet (ﷺ) went out (of his house to the Mosque) and said, "The trade of alcohol has become illegal." [Al-Bukhari, Book 34, Hadith 173]

The sin of a person who sells a free man.

حَدَّثَنِي بِشْرُ بْنُ مَرْحُومٍ، حَدَّثَنَا يَحْيَى بْنُ سُلَيْمٍ، عَنْ إِسْمَاعِيلَ بْنِ أُمَيَّةَ، عَنْ سَعِيدِ بْنِ أَبِي سَعِيدٍ، عَنْ أَبِي هُرَيْرَةَ ـ رضى الله عنه ـ عَنِ النَّبِيِّ صلى الله عليه وسلم قَالَ " قَالَ اللَّهُ ثَلاَثَةٌ أَنَا خَصْمُهُمْ يَوْمَ الْقِيَامَةِ، رَجُلٌ أَعْطَى بِي ثُمَّ غَدَرَ، وَرَجُلٌ بَاعَ حُرًّا فَأَكَلَ ثَمَنَهُ، وَرَجُلٌ اسْتَأْجَرَ أَجِيرًا فَاسْتَوْفَى مِنْهُ، وَلَمْ يُعْطِ أَجْرَهُ ".

8-Narrated Abu Huraira:

The Prophet (ﷺ) said, "Allah says, 'I will be against three people on the Day of Resurrection: -1. One who makes a covenant in My Name, but he proves treacherous. -2. <u>One who sells a free person (as a slave) and eats the price</u>, -3. And one who employs a laborer and gets the full work done by him but does not pay him his wages.' " [Al-Bukhari, Book 34, Hadith 174]

The sale of dead animals and idols

حَدَّثَنَا قُتَيْبَةُ، حَدَّثَنَا اللَّيْثُ، عَنْ يَزِيدَ بْنِ أَبِي حَبِيبٍ، عَنْ عَطَاءِ بْنِ أَبِي رَبَاحٍ، عَنْ جَابِرِ بْنِ عَبْدِ اللَّهِ ـ رضى الله عنهما ـ أَنَّهُ سَمِعَ رَسُولَ اللَّهِ صلى الله عليه وسلم يَقُولُ عَامَ الْفَتْحِ، وَهُوَ بِمَكَّةَ " إِنَّ اللَّهَ وَرَسُولَهُ حَرَّمَ بَيْعَ الْخَمْرِ وَالْمَيْتَةِ وَالْخِنْزِيرِ وَالأَصْنَامِ ". فَقِيلَ يَا رَسُولَ اللَّهِ، أَرَأَيْتَ شُحُومَ الْمَيْتَةِ فَإِنَّهَا يُطْلَى بِهَا السُّفُنُ، وَيُدْهَنُ بِهَا الْجُلُودُ، وَيَسْتَصْبِحُ بِهَا النَّاسُ. فَقَالَ " لاَ، هُوَ حَرَامٌ ". ثُمَّ قَالَ رَسُولُ اللَّهِ صلى الله عليه وسلم عِنْدَ ذَلِكَ " قَاتَلَ اللَّهُ الْيَهُودَ، إِنَّ اللَّهَ لَمَّا حَرَّمَ شُحُومَهَا جَمَلُوهُ ثُمَّ بَاعُوهُ فَأَكَلُوا ثَمَنَهُ ". قَالَ أَبُو عَاصِمٍ حَدَّثَنَا عَبْدُ الْحَمِيدِ، حَدَّثَنَا يَزِيدُ، كَتَبَ إِلَىَّ عَطَاءٌ سَمِعْتُ جَابِرًا ـ رضى الله عنه ـ عَنِ النَّبِيِّ صلى الله عليه وسلم.

9-Narrated Jabir bin `Abdullah:

I heard Allah's Messenger (ﷺ), in the year of the Conquest of Mecca, saying, <u>"Allah and His Apostle made illegal the trade of alcohol, dead animals, pigs, and idols."</u> The people asked, "O Allah's Messenger (ﷺ)! What about the <u>fat of dead animals, for it was</u>

used for greasing the boats and the hides; and people use it for lights?" He said, "No, it is illegal." Allah's Messenger (ﷺ) further said, "May Allah curse the Jews, for Allah, made the fat (of animals) illegal for them, yet they melted the fat and sold it and ate its price." [Al-Bukhari, Book 34, Hadith 182]

Price of a dog, tattoos, prostitution, interest, and soothsayer

حَدَّثَنَا عَبْدُ اللهِ بْنُ يُوسُفَ، أَخْبَرَنَا مَالِكٌ، عَنِ ابْنِ شِهَابٍ، عَنْ أَبِي بَكْرِ بْنِ عَبْدِ الرَّحْمَنِ، عَنْ أَبِي مَسْعُودٍ الأَنْصَارِيِّ ـ رضى الله عنه أَنَّ رَسُولَ اللَّهِ صلى الله عليه وسلم نَهَى عَنْ ثَمَنِ الْكَلْبِ وَمَهْرِ الْبَغِيِّ وَحُلْوَانِ الْكَاهِنِ.

10-Narrated Abu Mas`ud Al-Ansari:

Allah's Messenger (ﷺ) forbade taking the price of a dog, money earned by prostitution and the earnings of a soothsayer. [Al-Bukhari, Book 34, Hadith 183]

حَدَّثَنَا حَجَّاجُ بْنُ مِنْهَالٍ، حَدَّثَنَا شُعْبَةُ، قَالَ أَخْبَرَنِي عَوْنُ بْنُ أَبِي جُحَيْفَةَ، قَالَ رَأَيْتُ أَبِي اشْتَرَى حَجَّامًا، فَسَأَلْتُهُ عَنْ ذَلِكَ، قَالَ إِنَّ رَسُولَ اللَّهِ صلى الله عليه وسلم نَهَى عَنْ ثَمَنِ الدَّمِ، وَثَمَنِ الْكَلْبِ، وَكَسْبِ الأَمَةِ، وَلَعَنَ الْوَاشِمَةَ وَالْمُسْتَوْشِمَةَ، وَآكِلَ الرِّبَا، وَمُوكِلَهُ، وَلَعَنَ الْمُصَوِّرَ.

11-Narrated `Aun bin Abu Juhaifa:

I saw my father buying a slave whose profession was cupping and ordered that his instruments (of cupping) be broken. I asked him the reason for doing so. He replied, "Allah's Messenger (ﷺ) prohibited taking money for blood, the price of a dog, <u>and the earnings of a slave-girl by prostitution;</u> <u>he cursed her who tattoos and her who gets tattooed</u> the eater of Riba (usury), and the <u>maker of pictures</u>." [Al-Bukhari, Book 34, Hadith 184]

حَدَّثَنَا عَبْدُ اللَّهِ بْنُ يُوسُفَ، أَخْبَرَنَا مَالِكٌ، عَنْ نَافِعٍ، عَنِ الْقَاسِمِ بْنِ مُحَمَّدٍ، عَنْ عَائِشَةَ أُمِّ الْمُؤْمِنِينَ ـ رضى الله عنها ـ أَنَّهَا أَخْبَرَتْهُ أَنَّهَا اشْتَرَتْ نُمْرُقَةً فِيهَا تَصَاوِيرُ، فَلَمَّا رَآهَا رَسُولُ اللَّهِ صلى الله عليه وسلم قَامَ عَلَى الْبَابِ، فَلَمْ يَدْخُلْهُ، فَعَرَفْتُ فِي وَجْهِهِ الْكَرَاهِيَةَ، فَقُلْتُ يَا رَسُولَ اللَّهِ، أَتُوبُ إِلَى اللَّهِ وَإِلَى رَسُولِهِ صلى الله عليه وسلم مَاذَا أَذْنَبْتُ فَقَالَ رَسُولُ اللَّهِ صلى الله عليه وسلم سَدَهَا. فَقَالَ " مَا بَالُ هَذِهِ النُّمْرُقَةِ ". قُلْتُ اشْتَرَيْتُهَا لَكَ لِتَقْعُدَ عَلَيْهَا وَتَوَ رَسُولُ اللَّهِ صلى الله عليه وسلم " إِنَّ أَصْحَابَ هَذِهِ الصُّوَرِ يَوْمَ الْقِيَامَةِ يُعَذَّبُونَ، فَيُقَالُ لَهُمْ أَحْيُوا مَا خَلَقْتُمْ ". وَقَالَ " إِنَّ الْبَيْتَ الَّذِي فِيهِ الصُّوَرُ لاَ تَدْخُلُهُ الْمَلاَئِكَةُ ".

12-Narrated Aisha:

(mother of the faithful believers) I bought a cushion with pictures on it. When Allah's Messenger (ﷺ) saw it, he kept standing at the door and did not enter the house. I noticed the sign of disgust on his face, so I said, "O Allah's Messenger (ﷺ)! I repent to Allah and His Apostle. (Please let me know) what sin I have done." Allah's Messenger (ﷺ) said, "What about this cushion?" I replied, "I bought it for you to sit and recline on." Allah's Messenger (ﷺ) said,

"The painters (i.e. owners) of these pictures will be punished on the Day of Resurrection. It will be said to them, 'Put life in what you have created (i.e. painted).'" The Prophet (ﷺ) added, "The angels do not enter a house where there are pictures." [Al-Bukhari, Book 34, Hadith 58]

Al-gharar and herbal-il-habala

حَدَّثَنَا عَبْدُ اللَّهِ بْنُ يُوسُفَ، أَخْبَرَنَا مَالِكٌ، عَنْ نَافِعٍ، عَنْ عَبْدِ اللَّهِ بْنِ عُمَرَ ـ رضى الله عنهما ـ أَنَّ رَسُولَ اللَّهِ صلى الله عليه وسلم نَهَى عَنْ بَيْعِ حَبَلِ الْحَبَلَةِ، وَكَانَ بَيْعًا يَتَبَايَعُهُ أَهْلُ الْجَاهِلِيَّةِ، كَانَ الرَّجُلُ يَبْتَاعُ الْجَزُورَ إِلَى أَنْ تُنْتَجَ النَّاقَةُ، ثُمَّ تُنْتَجَ الَّتِي فِي بَطْنِهَا.

13-Narrated `Abdullah bin `Umar:

Allah's Messenger (ﷺ) forbade the sale called 'Habal-al-Habala which was a kind of sale practiced in the Pre- Islamic Period of ignorance. One would pay the price of a she-camel which was not born yet would be borne by the immediate offspring of an extant she-camel. [Al-Bukhari, Book 34, Hadith 95]

Selling of silver for gold on delayed payment

حَدَّثَنَا حَفْصُ بْنُ عُمَرَ، حَدَّثَنَا شُعْبَةُ، قَالَ أَخْبَرَنِي حَبِيبُ بْنُ أَبِي ثَابِتٍ، قَالَ سَمِعْتُ أَبَا الْمِنْهَالِ، قَالَ سَأَلْتُ الْبَرَاءَ بْنَ عَازِبٍ وَزَيْدَ بْنَ أَرْقَمَ ـ رضى الله عنهم ـ عَنِ الصَّرْفِ،، فَكُلُّ وَاحِدٍ مِنْهُمَا يَقُولُ هَذَا خَيْرٌ مِنِّي. فَكِلَاهُمَا يَقُولُ

نَهَى رَسُولُ اللَّهِ صلى الله عليه وسلم عَنْ بَيْعِ الذَّهَبِ بِالْوَرِقِ دَيْنًا.

14-Narrated Abu Al-Minhal:

I asked Albara' bin `Azib and Zaid bin Arqam about money exchanges. Each of them said, "This is better than I," and both of them said, "Allah's Messenger (ﷺ) forbade the selling of silver for gold on credit. " [Al-Bukhari, Book 34, Hadith 129/ 2180, 2181]

Silk as a product

حَدَّثَنَا آدَمُ، حَدَّثَنَا شُعْبَةُ، حَدَّثَنَا أَبُو بَكْرِ بْنُ حَفْصٍ، عَنْ سَالِمِ بْنِ عَبْدِ اللَّهِ بْنِ عُمَرَ، عَنْ أَبِيهِ، قَالَ أَرْسَلَ النَّبِيُّ صلى الله عليه وسلم إِلَى عُمَرَ ـ رضى الله عنه ـ بِحُلَّةِ حَرِيرٍ ـ أَوْ سِيَرَاءَ ـ فَرَآهَا عَلَيْهِ، فَقَالَ " إِنِّي لَمْ أُرْسِلْ بِهَا إِلَيْكَ لِتَلْبَسَهَا، إِنَّمَا يَلْبَسُهَا مَنْ لاَ خَلاَقَ لَهُ، إِنَّمَا بَعَثْتُ إِلَيْكَ لِتَسْتَمْتِعَ بِهَا ". يَعْنِي تَبِيعُهَا.

15-Narrated `Abdullah bin `Umar:

Once the Prophet (ﷺ) sent Umar a silken two-piece garment to him, and when he saw `Umar wearing it, he said to him, "I have not sent it to you to wear it. It is worn by him who has no share in the Hereafter, and I have sent it to you so that you could receive help from it (i.e., sell it). [Al-Bukhari, Book 34, Hadith 57]

C-DOUBTFUL PRODUCTS

حَدَّثَنِي مُحَمَّدُ بْنُ الْمُثَنَّى، حَدَّثَنَا ابْنُ أَبِي عَدِيٍّ، عَنِ ابْنِ عَوْنٍ، عَنِ الشَّعْبِيِّ، سَمِعْتُ النُّعْمَانَ بْنَ بَشِيرٍ ـ رضى الله عنه ـ سَمِعْتُ النَّبِيَّ صلى الله عليه وسلم. حَدَّثَنَا عَلِيُّ بْنُ عَبْدِ اللَّهِ، حَدَّثَنَا ابْنُ عُيَيْنَةَ، عَنْ أَبِي فَرْوَةَ، عَنِ الشَّعْبِيِّ، قَالَ سَمِعْتُ النُّعْمَانَ، عَنِ النَّبِيِّ صلى الله عليه وسلم. حَدَّثَنَا عَبْدُ اللَّهِ بْنُ مُحَمَّدٍ، حَدَّثَنَا ابْنُ عُيَيْنَةَ، عَنْ أَبِي فَرْوَةَ، سَمِعْتُ الشَّعْبِيَّ، سَمِعْتُ النُّعْمَانَ بْنَ بَشِيرٍ ـ رضى الله عنهما ـ عَنِ النَّبِيِّ صلى الله عليه وسلم. حَدَّثَنَا مُحَمَّدُ بْنُ كَثِيرٍ، أَخْبَرَنَا سُفْيَانُ، عَنْ أَبِي فَرْوَةَ، عَنِ الشَّعْبِيِّ، عَنِ النُّعْمَانِ بْنِ بَشِيرٍ ـ رضى الله عنه ـ قَالَ قَالَ النَّبِيُّ صلى الله عليه وسلم " الْحَلاَلُ بَيِّنٌ، وَالْحَرَامُ بَيِّنٌ وَبَيْنَهُمَا أُمُورٌ مُشْتَبِهَةٌ، فَمَنْ تَرَكَ مَا شُبِّهَ عَلَيْهِ مِنَ الإِثْمِ كَانَ لِمَا اسْتَبَانَ أَتْرَكَ، وَمَنِ اجْتَرَأَ عَلَى مَا يَشُكُّ فِيهِ مِنَ الإِثْمِ أَوْشَكَ أَنْ يُوَاقِعَ مَا اسْتَبَانَ، وَالْمَعَاصِي حِمَى اللَّهِ، مَنْ يَرْتَعْ حَوْلَ الْحِمَى يُوشِكُ أَنْ يُوَاقِعَهُ ".

16-Narrated An-Nu`man bin Bashir:

The Prophet (ﷺ) said "Both legal and illegal things are obvious, and in between, they are (suspicious) doubtful matters. So, whoever forsakes those doubtful things lest he may commit a sin, will avoid what is clearly illegal; and whoever indulges in these (suspicious) doubtful things bravely, is likely to commit what is clearly illegal. <u>Sins are Allah's Hima (i.e. private pasture) and whoever pastures (his sheep) near it, is likely to get in it at any moment.</u>"
[Al-Bukhari Book 34, Hadith 5]

4 PROCESS

INTRODUCTION

A process is a way by which exchange of goods and services are made. There are thirty-three ahadith in the chapter and eleven sub-sections. The starting point is leniency in dealing i.e., buying, selling, and demanding credit. Generosity in all occupations is an Islamic character; it is especially crucial when seller demands money for the credit sales.

In this connection, cash sales are praised in some cases than the credit sales. For instance, silver for gold. However, the prophet (ﷺ) bought she-camel on delayed payment of Abu Bakr at the occasion of Hijrah. In addition, al-gharer and mulamasa transactions were declared unlawful. A seller confirms the value of his product through swearing which generates the confidence of the potential buyer. Swearing could be true or otherwise, therefore, it is not desirable. Similarly, some sort of barter transactions are not permissible. The purpose is to protect the rights of the parties involved. Some barters benefit seller and some of them to the buyer. For instance, fresh dates are not allowed to barter with dried dates. Exchange of good quality data (product) is also not desirable with low quality dates. It applies to other products as well. While generating a transaction, the seller needs to tell the defects of the product he is offering. Men cannot wear silk, women can but its transaction is halal. A similar ruling applies to gold.

Araya transaction is allowed for a given quantity. However, the writer of Tofatul-Qari concluded that it is permissible because araya trees were a gift of the owner of the garden. When the person to whom the tree(s) were gifted visited the trees while the dates were not ready. The owner sometimes did not like it because his family used to be there as well. Therefore, he used to buy it for dried dates. The price was paid by estimating the fruit of the gifted trees. Therefore, it was a kind of sale from the seller point of view.

A-LENIENCY IN BARGAINING

حَدَّثَنَا عَلِيُّ بْنُ عَيَّاشٍ، حَدَّثَنَا أَبُو غَسَّانَ، مُحَمَّدُ بْنُ مُطَرِّفٍ قَالَ حَدَّثَنِي مُحَمَّدُ

بْنُ الْمُنْكَدِرِ، عَنْ جَابِرِ بْنِ عَبْدِ اللَّهِ ـ رضى الله عنهما ـ أَنَّ رَسُولَ اللَّهِ صلى الله عليه وسلم قَالَ " رَحِمَ اللَّهُ رَجُلاً سَمْحًا إِذَا بَاعَ، وَإِذَا اشْتَرَى، وَإِذَا اقْتَضَى ".

1-Narrated Jabir bin `Abdullah:

Allah's Messenger (ﷺ) said, "May Allah's mercy be on him who is lenient in his buying, selling, and in demanding back his money." [Al-Bukhari, Book 34, Hadith 29]

حَدَّثَنَا أَحْمَدُ بْنُ يُونُسَ، حَدَّثَنَا زُهَيْرٌ، حَدَّثَنَا مَنْصُورٌ، أَنَّ رِبْعِيَّ بْنَ حِرَاشٍ، حَدَّثَهُ أَنَّ حُذَيْفَةَ ـ رضى الله عنه ـ حَدَّثَهُ قَالَ قَالَ النَّبِيُّ صلى الله عليه وسلم " تَلَقَّتِ الْمَلاَئِكَةُ رُوحَ رَجُلٍ مِمَّنْ كَانَ قَبْلَكُمْ قَالُوا أَعَمِلْتَ مِنَ الْخَيْرِ شَيْئًا قَالَ كُنْتُ آمُرُ فِتْيَانِي أَنْ يُنْظِرُوا وَيَتَجَاوَزُوا عَنِ الْمُوسِرِ قَالَ قَالَ فَتَجَاوَزُوا عَنْهُ ". وَقَالَ أَبُو مَالِكٍ عَنْ رِبْعِيٍّ " كُنْتُ أُيَسِّرُ عَلَى الْمُوسِرِ وَأُنْظِرُ الْمُعْسِرَ ". وَتَابَعَهُ شُعْبَةُ عَنْ عَبْدِ الْمَلِكِ عَنْ رِبْعِيٍّ. وَقَالَ أَبُو عَوَانَةَ عَنْ عَبْدِ الْمَلِكِ عَنْ رِبْعِيٍّ " أُنْظِرُ الْمُوسِرَ، وَأَتَجَاوَزُ عَنِ الْمُعْسِرِ ". وَقَالَ نُعَيْمُ بْنُ أَبِي هِنْدٍ عَنْ رِبْعِيٍّ " فَأَقْبَلُ مِنَ الْمُوسِرِ، وَأَتَجَاوَزُ عَنِ الْمُعْسِرِ ".

2-Narrated Hudhaifa:

The Prophet (ﷺ) said, "Before your time the angels received the soul of a man and asked him, 'Did you do any good deeds (in your life)?' He replied, 'I used to order my employees to grant time to the rich person to pay his debts at his convenience.' So, Allah said to the angels; "Excuse him." Rabi said that (the dead man said), 'I used to be easy to the rich and grant time to the poor.' Or, in another narration, 'grant time to the well-off and forgive the needy,' or 'accept from the well-off and forgive the needy.' [Al-Bukhari, Book 34, Hadith 30]

حَدَّثَنَا هِشَامُ بْنُ عَمَّارٍ، حَدَّثَنَا يَحْيَى بْنُ حَمْزَةَ، حَدَّثَنَا الزُّبَيْدِيُّ، عَنِ الزُّهْرِيِّ، عَنْ عُبَيْدِ اللَّهِ بْنِ عَبْدِ اللَّهِ، أَنَّهُ سَمِعَ أَبَا هُرَيْرَةَ ـ رضى الله عنه ـ عَنِ النَّبِيِّ صلى الله عليه وسلم قَالَ " كَانَ تَاجِرٌ يُدَايِنُ النَّاسَ، فَإِذَا رَأَى مُعْسِرًا قَالَ لِفِتْيَانِهِ تَجَاوَزُوا عَنْهُ، لَعَلَّ اللَّهَ أَنْ يَتَجَاوَزَ عَنَّا، فَتَجَاوَزَ اللَّهُ عَنْهُ ".

3-Narrated Abu Huraira:

The Prophet (ﷺ) said, "There was a merchant who used to lend the people, and whenever his debtor was in straitened circumstances, he would say to his employees, 'Forgive him so that Allah may forgive us.' So, Allah forgave him." [Al-Bukhari, Book 34, Hadith 31]

B-POSSESSION OF PRODUCT

حَدَّثَنَا إِبْرَاهِيمُ بْنُ الْمُنْذِرِ، حَدَّثَنَا أَبُو ضَمْرَةَ، حَدَّثَنَا مُوسَى، عَنْ نَافِعٍ، حَدَّثَنَا ابْنُ عُمَرَ، أَنَّهُمْ كَانُوا يَشْتَرُونَ الطَّعَامَ مِنَ الرُّكْبَانِ عَلَى عَهْدِ النَّبِيِّ صلى الله عليه وسلم فَيَبْعَثُ عَلَيْهِمْ مَنْ يَمْنَعُهُمْ أَنْ يَبِيعُوهُ حَيْثُ اشْتَرَوْهُ، حَتَّى يَنْقُلُوهُ حَيْثُ يُبَاعُ الطَّعَامُ. قَالَ وَحَدَّثَنَا ابْنُ عُمَرَ ـ رضى الله عنهما ـ قَالَ نَهَى النَّبِيُّ صلى الله عليه وسلم أَنْ يُبَاعَ الطَّعَامُ إِذَا اشْتَرَاهُ حَتَّى يَسْتَوْفِيَهُ.

4-Narrated Nafi`:

Ibn `Umar told us that the people used to buy food

from the caravans in the lifetime of the Prophet. <u>The Prophet (ﷺ) used to forbid them to sell it at the very place where they had bought it (but they were to wait) till they carried it to the market where foodstuff was sold.</u> Ibn `Umar said, 'The Prophet (ﷺ) also forbade the reselling of foodstuff by somebody who had bought it unless he had received it with exact full measure.' [Al-Bukhari, Book 34, Hadith 76]

C-CASH / CREDIT SALES

حَدَّثَنَا بِشْرُ بْنُ مُحَمَّدٍ، أَخْبَرَنَا عَبْدُ اللَّهِ، أَخْبَرَنَا الْحُسَيْنُ الْمُكْتِبُ، عَنْ عَطَاءِ بْنِ أَبِي رَبَاحٍ، عَنْ جَابِرِ بْنِ عَبْدِ اللَّهِ ـ رضى الله عنهما ـ أَنَّ رَجُلاً أَعْتَقَ غُلاَمًا لَهُ عَنْ دُبُرٍ، فَاحْتَاجَ فَأَخَذَهُ النَّبِيُّ صلى الله عليه وسلم فَقَالَ " مَنْ يَشْتَرِيهِ مِنِّي " فَاشْتَرَاهُ نُعَيْمُ بْنُ عَبْدِ اللَّهِ بِكَذَا وَكَذَا، فَدَفَعَهُ إِلَيْهِ.

5-Narrated Jabir bin `Abdullah:

A man decided that a slave of his would be manumitted after his death and later on he was in need of money, so the Prophet (ﷺ) took the slave and said, "<u>Who will buy this slave from me?" Nu'aim bin `Abdullah bought him for such and such price and the Prophet (ﷺ) gave him the slave.</u> [Al-Bukhari, Book 34, Hadith 93/2141]

حَدَّثَنَا حَفْصُ بْنُ عُمَرَ، حَدَّثَنَا شُعْبَةُ، قَالَ أَخْبَرَنِي حَبِيبُ بْنُ أَبِي ثَابِتٍ، قَالَ سَمِعْتُ أَبَا الْمِنْهَالِ، قَالَ سَأَلْتُ الْبَرَاءَ بْنَ عَازِبٍ وَزَيْدَ بْنَ أَرْقَمَ ـ رضى الله عنهم ـ عَنِ الصَّرْفِ، فَكُلُّ وَاحِدٍ مِنْهُمَا يَقُولُ هَذَا خَيْرٌ مِنِّي. فَكِلاَهُمَا يَقُولُ نَهَى

رَسُولُ اللَّهِ صلى الله عليه وسلم عَنْ بَيْعِ الذَّهَبِ بِالْوَرِقِ دَيْنًا.

6-Narrated Abu Al-Minhal:

I asked Albara' bin `Azib and Zaid bin Arqam about money exchanges. Each of them said, "This is better than I," and both of them said, "Allah's Messenger (ﷺ) forbade the selling of silver for gold on credit." [Al-Bukhari, Book 34, Hadith 129/ 2180, 2181]

D-AL-GHARER TRANSACTIONS

It implies conditional transactions. People used to do it in the pre-Islamic period i.e. I will pay the price provided a certain condition would occur. For example, I will pay the price if this she-camel would give birth of a calf. It implies that the buyer would pay if he received a particular benefit i.e., a calf out of the she-camel. It may be exemplified through another condition that someone is buying a capital good (a machine, taxi, van etc.) and stipulates that he will pay price if he earns a profit. Based on this and other ahadith, Mufti Taqi Sahib concludes that al-gharer is haram (p. 274). (Allah knows better)

حَدَّثَنَا عَبْدُ اللَّهِ بْنُ يُوسُفَ، أَخْبَرَنَا مَالِكٌ، عَنْ نَافِعٍ، عَنْ عَبْدِ اللَّهِ بْنِ عُمَرَ ـ رضى الله عنهما ـ أَنَّ رَسُولَ اللَّهِ صلى الله عليه وسلم نَهَى عَنْ بَيْعِ حَبَلِ الْحَبَلَةِ، وَكَانَ بَيْعًا يَتَبَايَعُهُ أَهْلُ الْجَاهِلِيَّةِ، كَانَ الرَّجُلُ يَبْتَاعُ الْجَزُورَ إِلَى أَنْ تُنْتَجَ النَّاقَةُ، ثُمَّ تُنْتَجُ الَّتِي فِي بَطْنِهَا.

7-Narrated `Abdullah bin `Umar:

Allah's Messenger (ﷺ) forbade the sale called 'Habal-al-Habala which was a kind of sale practiced in the Pre- Islamic Period of ignorance. <u>One would pay the price of a she-camel which was not born yet would be borne by the immediate offspring of an extant she-camel.</u> [Al-Bukhari, Book 34, Hadith 95/2143]

E-AL-LIMAS OR MULAMASA (EXAMINATION OF PRODUCT)

حَدَّثَنَا سَعِيدُ بْنُ عُفَيْرٍ، قَالَ حَدَّثَنِي اللَّيْثُ، قَالَ حَدَّثَنِي عُقَيْلٌ، عَنِ ابْنِ شِهَابٍ، قَالَ أَخْبَرَنِي عَامِرُ بْنُ سَعْدٍ، أَنَّ أَبَا سَعِيدٍ ـ رضى الله عنه ـ أَخْبَرَهُ أَنَّ رَسُولَ اللَّهِ صلى الله عليه وسلم نَهَى عَنِ الْمُنَابَذَةِ، وَهْىَ طَرْحُ الرَّجُلِ ثَوْبَهُ بِالْبَيْعِ إِلَى الرَّجُلِ، قَبْلَ أَنْ يُقَلِّبَهُ، أَوْ يَنْظُرَ إِلَيْهِ، وَنَهَى عَنِ الْمُلاَمَسَةِ، وَالْمُلاَمَسَةُ لَمْسُ الثَّوْبِ لاَ يَنْظُرُ إِلَيْهِ.

8-Narrated Abu Sa`id:

Allah's Messenger (ﷺ) forbade the selling by Munabadha, i.e. <u>to sell one's garment by casting it to the buyer not allowing him to examine or see it. Similarly</u>, he <u>forbade</u> the selling by Mulamasa. Mulamasa is to buy a garment, for example, <u>by merely touching it, not looking at it.</u> [Al-Bukhari, Book 34, Hadith 96/2144]

حَدَّثَنَا قُتَيْبَةُ، حَدَّثَنَا عَبْدُ الْوَهَّابِ، حَدَّثَنَا أَيُّوبُ، عَنْ مُحَمَّدٍ، عَنْ أَبِي هُرَيْرَةَ ـ رضى الله عنه ـ قَالَ نُهِيَ عَنْ لِبْسَتَيْنِ، أَنْ يَحْتَبِيَ الرَّجُلُ، فِي الثَّوْبِ الْوَاحِدِ، ثُمَّ يَرْفَعَهُ عَلَى مَنْكِبِهِ، وَعَنْ بَيْعَتَيْنِ اللِّمَاسِ وَالنِّبَاذِ.

9-Narrated Abu Huraira:

The Prophet (ﷺ) forbade two kinds of dressing; (one of them) is to sit with one's legs drawn up while wrapped in one garment. (The other) is to lift that garment on one's shoulders. <u>And forbade two kinds of sale: Al-Limais and An-Nibadh.</u> [Al-Bukhari, Book 34, Hadith 97]

F-SWEARING

حَدَّثَنَا عَمْرُو بْنُ مُحَمَّدٍ، حَدَّثَنَا هُشَيْمٌ، أَخْبَرَنَا الْعَوَّامُ، عَنْ إِبْرَاهِيمَ بْنِ عَبْدِ الرَّحْمَنِ، عَنْ عَبْدِ اللَّهِ بْنِ أَبِي أَوْفَى ـ رضى الله عنه ـ أَنَّ رَجُلاً، أَقَامَ سِلْعَةً، وَهُوَ فِي السُّوقِ، فَحَلَفَ بِاللَّهِ لَقَدْ أَعْطَى بِهَا مَا لَمْ يُعْطَ، لِيُوقِعَ فِيهَا رَجُلاً مِنَ الْمُسْلِمِينَ، فَنَزَلَتْ ﴿إِنَّ الَّذِينَ يَشْتَرُونَ بِعَهْدِ اللَّهِ وَأَيْمَانِهِمْ ثَمَنًا قَلِيلاً﴾

10-Narrated `Abdullah bin Abu `Aufa:

<u>A man displayed some goods in the market and swore by Allah that he had been offered so much for that, that which was not offered, and he said so, to cheat a Muslim.</u> On that occasion, the following Verse was revealed: "Verily! Those who buy a small gain at the cost of Allah's covenant and their oaths (They shall have no part in the Hereafter...etc.)' (3.77) [Al-Bukhari, Book 34, Hadith 41]

G-BARTER

حَدَّثَنَا عَلِيٌّ، حَدَّثَنَا سُفْيَانُ، كَانَ عَمْرُو بْنُ دِينَارٍ يُحَدِّثُهُ عَنِ الزُّهْرِيِّ، عَنْ مَالِكِ بْنِ أَوْسٍ، أَنَّهُ قَالَ مَنْ عِنْدَهُ صَرْفٌ فَقَالَ طَلْحَةُ أَنَا حَتَّى يَجِيءَ خَازِنُنَا مِنَ الْغَابَةِ. قَالَ سُفْيَانُ هُوَ الَّذِي حَفِظْنَاهُ مِنَ الزُّهْرِيِّ لَيْسَ فِيهِ زِيَادَةٌ. فَقَالَ أَخْبَرَنِي مَالِكُ بْنُ أَوْسٍ سَمِعَ عُمَرَ بْنَ الْخَطَّابِ ـ رضى الله عنه ـ يُخْبِرُ عَنْ رَسُولِ اللَّهِ صلى الله عليه وسلم قَالَ " الذَّهَبُ بِالذَّهَبِ رِبًا إِلاَّ هَاءَ وَهَاءَ، وَالْبُرُّ بِالْبُرِّ رِبًا إِلاَّ هَاءَ وَهَاءَ، وَالتَّمْرُ بِالتَّمْرِ رِبًا إِلاَّ هَاءَ وَهَاءَ، وَالشَّعِيرُ بِالشَّعِيرِ رِبًا إِلاَّ هَاءَ وَهَاءَ ".

11-Narrated Az-Zuhri from Malik bin Aus:

That the latter said, "Who has changed?" Talha said, "I (will have change) when our storekeeper comes from the forest." Malik bin Aus narrated from `Umar bin Al-Khattab: Allah's Messenger (ﷺ) said, "The bartering of gold for gold is <u>Riba (usury)</u>, except if it is from hand to hand and equal in amount, and wheat grain for wheat grain is usury except if it is formed hand to hand and equal in amount, and dates for dates is usury except if it is from hand to hand and equal in amount, and barley for barley is usury except if it is from hand to hand and equal in amount." [Al-Bukhari, Book 34, Hadith 86]

Barter (illegal): selling of dates for dates.

حَدَّثَنَا أَبُو الْوَلِيدِ، حَدَّثَنَا اللَّيْثُ، عَنِ ابْنِ شِهَابٍ، عَنْ مَالِكِ بْنِ أَوْسٍ، سَمِعَ عُمَرَ

ـ رضى الله عنهما ـ عَنِ النَّبِيِّ صلى الله عليه وسلم قَالَ " الْبُرُّ بِالْبُرِّ رِبًا إِلاَّ هَاءَ وَهَاءَ، وَالشَّعِيرُ بِالشَّعِيرِ رِبًا إِلاَّ هَاءَ وَهَاءَ، وَالتَّمْرُ بِالتَّمْرِ رِبًا إِلاَّ هَاءَ وَهَاءَ ".

12-Narrated Ibn `Umar:

The Prophet (ﷺ) said, "The selling of wheat for wheat is Riba (usury) except if it is handed from hand to hand and equal in amount. Similarly, the selling of barley for barley is Riba except if it is from hand to hand and equal in amount, and dates for dates are usury except if it is from hand to hand and equal in amount. (See Riba-Fadl in the glossary). [Al-Bukhari, Book 34, Hadith 121]

حَدَّثَنَا إِسْمَاعِيلُ، حَدَّثَنَا مَالِكٌ، عَنْ نَافِعٍ، عَنْ عَبْدِ اللَّهِ بْنِ عُمَرَ ـ رضى الله عنهما ـ أَنَّ رَسُولَ اللَّهِ صلى الله عليه وسلم نَهَى عَنِ الْمُزَابَنَةِ، وَالْمُزَابَنَةُ بَيْعُ التَّمْرِ بِالتَّمْرِ كَيْلاً، وَبَيْعُ الزَّبِيبِ بِالْكَرْمِ كَيْلاً.

13-Narrated Ibn `Umar:

Allah's Messenger (ﷺ) forbade Muzabana, and Muzabana is the selling of fresh dates for dried old dates by measure, and the selling of fresh grapes for dried grapes by measure. [Al-Bukhari, Book 34, Hadith 122]

حَدَّثَنَا أَبُو النُّعْمَانِ، حَدَّثَنَا حَمَّادُ بْنُ زَيْدٍ، عَنْ أَيُّوبَ، عَنْ نَافِعٍ، عَنِ ابْنِ عُمَرَ ـ رضى الله عنهما ـ أَنَّ النَّبِيَّ صلى الله عليه وسلم نَهَى عَنِ الْمُزَابَنَةِ قَالَ وَالْمُزَابَنَةُ أَنْ يَبِيعَ التَّمْرَ بِكَيْلٍ، إِنْ زَادَ فَلِي وَإِنْ نَقَصَ فَعَلَىَّ. قَالَ وَحَدَّثَنِي زَيْدُ

بْنُ ثَابِتٍ، أَنَّ النَّبِيَّ صلى الله عليه وسلم رَخَّصَ فِي الْعَرَايَا بِخَرْصِهَا.

14-Narrated Ibn `Umar:

The Prophet (ﷺ) forbade Muzabana; and Muzabana is the selling of fresh fruit (without measuring it) for something by measure on the basis that if that thing turns to be more than the fruit, <u>the increase would be for the seller of the fruit, and if it turns to be less, that would be of his lot</u>. Narrated Ibn `Umar from Zaid bin Thabit that the <u>Prophet (ﷺ) allowed the selling of the fruits on the trees after estimation (when they are ripe)</u>. [Al-Bukhari, Book 34, Hadith 123]

Illegal bargain (riba) barley for barley

15-Narrated Ibn Shihab:

that Malik bin Aus said, "I was in need of change for one-hundred Dinars. Talha bin 'Ubaidullah called me and we discussed the matter, and he agreed to change (my Dinars). He took the gold pieces in his hands and fidgeted with them, and then said, "Wait till my storekeeper comes from the forest." `Umar was listening to that and said, "By Allah! You should not separate from Talha till you get the money from him, for Allah's Messenger (ﷺ) said, 'The selling of gold for gold is Riba (usury) except if the exchange is from hand to hand and equal in amount, and similarly, the selling of wheat for wheat is Riba (usury) unless it is from hand to hand and equal in amount, and the selling of barley for barley is usury unless it is from hand to hand and equal in amount, and dates for dates, is usury unless it is from hand to hand and equal in amount" [Al-Bukhari, Book 34, Hadith 124] Hadith 121 is similar to it

Selling of gold for gold

حَدَّثَنَا صَدَقَةُ بْنُ الْفَضْلِ، أَخْبَرَنَا إِسْمَاعِيلُ ابْنُ عُلَيَّةَ، قَالَ حَدَّثَنِي يَحْيَى بْنُ أَبِي إِسْحَاقَ، حَدَّثَنَا عَبْدُ الرَّحْمَنِ بْنُ أَبِي بَكْرَةَ، قَالَ قَالَ أَبُو بَكْرَةَ ـ رضى الله عنه ـ قَالَ رَسُولُ اللَّهِ صلى الله عليه وسلم " لاَ تَبِيعُوا الذَّهَبَ بِالذَّهَبِ إِلاَّ سَوَاءً بِسَوَاءٍ، وَالْفِضَّةَ بِالْفِضَّةِ إِلاَّ سَوَاءً بِسَوَاءٍ، وَبِيعُوا الذَّهَبَ بِالْفِضَّةِ وَالْفِضَّةَ بِالذَّهَبِ كَيْفَ شِئْتُمْ ".

17-Narrated Abu Bakra:

Allah's Messenger (ﷺ) said, "Don't sell gold for gold unless equal in weight, nor silver for silver unless equal in weight, but you could sell gold for silver or silver for gold as you like." [Al-Bukhari, Book 34, Hadith 125]

حَدَّثَنَا عَبْدُ اللَّهِ بْنُ يُوسُفَ، أَخْبَرَنَا مَالِكٌ، عَنْ نَافِعٍ، عَنْ أَبِي سَعِيدٍ الْخُدْرِيِّ ـ رضى الله عنه ـ أَنَّ رَسُولَ اللَّهِ صلى الله عليه وسلم قَالَ " لاَ تَبِيعُوا الذَّهَبَ بِالذَّهَبِ إِلاَّ مِثْلاً بِمِثْلٍ، وَلاَ تُشِفُّوا بَعْضَهَا عَلَى بَعْضٍ، وَلاَ تَبِيعُوا الْوَرِقَ

بِالْوَرِقِ إِلاَّ مِثْلاً بِمِثْلٍ، وَلاَ تُشِفُّوا بَعْضَهَا عَلَى بَعْضٍ، وَلاَ تَبِيعُوا مِنْهَا غَائِبًا بِنَاجِزٍ"

18-Narrated Abu Sa`id Al-Khudri:

Allah's Messenger (ﷺ) said, "Do not sell gold for gold unless equivalent in weight, and do not sell less amount for greater amount or vice versa; and do not sell silver for silver unless equivalent in weight, and do not sell less amount for greater amount or vice versa and <u>do not sell gold or silver that is not present at the moment of exchange for gold or silver that is present.</u> [Al-Bukhari, Book 34, Hadith 127]

Selling of Dinar for Dinar on credit

حَدَّثَنَا عَلِيُّ بْنُ عَبْدِ اللَّهِ، حَدَّثَنَا الضَّحَّاكُ بْنُ مَخْلَدٍ، حَدَّثَنَا ابْنُ جُرَيْجٍ، قَالَ أَخْبَرَنِي عَمْرُو بْنُ دِينَارٍ، أَنَّ أَبَا صَالِحٍ الزَّيَّاتَ، أَخْبَرَهُ أَنَّهُ، سَمِعَ أَبَا سَعِيدٍ الْخُدْرِيَّ ـ رضى الله عنه ـ يَقُولُ الدِّينَارُ بِالدِّينَارِ، وَالدِّرْهَمُ بِالدِّرْهَمِ. فَقُلْتُ لَهُ فَإِنَّ ابْنَ عَبَّاسٍ لاَ يَقُولُهُ. فَقَالَ أَبُو سَعِيدٍ سَأَلْتُهُ فَقُلْتُ سَمِعْتَهُ مِنَ النَّبِيِّ، صلى الله عليه وسلم، أَوْ وَجَدْتَهُ فِي كِتَابِ اللَّهِ قَالَ كُلُّ ذَلِكَ لاَ أَقُولُ، وَأَنْتُمْ أَعْلَمُ بِرَسُولِ اللَّهِ صلى الله عليه وسلم مِنِّي، وَلَكِنِّي أَخْبَرَنِي أُسَامَةُ أَنَّ النَّبِيَّ صلى الله عليه وسلم قَالَ " لاَ رِبًا إِلاَّ فِي النَّسِيئَةِ ".

19-Narrated Abu Salih Az-Zaiyat:

I heard Abu Sa`id Al-Khudri said, "The selling of a Dinar for a Dinar, and a Dirham for a Dirham (is permissible)." I said to him, "Ibn `Abbas does not say the same." Abu Sa`id replied, "I asked Ibn

`Abbas whether he had heard it from the Prophet (ﷺ) or seen it in the Holy Book. Ibn `Abbas replied, "I do not claim that, and you know Allah's Messenger (ﷺ) better than I, but Usama informed me that the Prophet (ﷺ) had said, 'There is no Riba (in money exchange) except when it is not done from hand to hand (i.e. when there is delay in payment).'" [Al-Bukhari, Book 34, Hadith 128] (Dose it the Mazhab of Jamhoor?)

Exchange of money on credit

حَدَّثَنَا أَبُو عَاصِمٍ، عَنِ ابْنِ جُرَيْجٍ، قَالَ أَخْبَرَنِي عَمْرُو بْنُ دِينَارٍ، عَنْ أَبِي الْمِنْهَالِ، قَالَ كُنْتُ أَتَّجِرُ فِي الصَّرْفِ، فَسَأَلْتُ زَيْدَ بْنَ أَرْقَمَ ـ رضى الله عنه ـ فَقَالَ قَالَ النَّبِيُّ صلى الله عليه وسلم. وَحَدَّثَنِي الْفَضْلُ بْنُ يَعْقُوبَ، حَدَّثَنَا الْحَجَّاجُ بْنُ مُحَمَّدٍ، قَالَ ابْنُ جُرَيْجٍ أَخْبَرَنِي عَمْرُو بْنُ دِينَارٍ، وَعَامِرُ بْنُ مُصْعَبٍ، أَنَّهُمَا سَمِعَا أَبَا الْمِنْهَالِ، يَقُولُ سَأَلْتُ الْبَرَاءَ بْنَ عَازِبٍ وَزَيْدَ بْنَ أَرْقَمَ عَنِ الصَّرْفِ، فَقَالاَ كُنَّا تَاجِرَيْنِ عَلَى عَهْدِ رَسُولِ اللَّهِ صلى الله عليه وسلم فَسَأَلْنَا رَسُولَ اللَّهِ صلى الله عليه وسلم عَنِ الصَّرْفِ فَقَالَ " إِنْ كَانَ يَدًا بِيَدٍ فَلاَ بَأْسَ، وَإِنْ كَانَ نَسَاءً فَلاَ يَصْلُحُ ".

20-Narrated Abu Al-Minhal:

I used to practice money exchange, and I asked Zaid bin 'Arqam about it, and he narrated what the Prophet said in the following: Abu Al-Minhal said, "I asked Al-Bara' bin `Azib and Zaid bin Arqam about practicing money exchange. They replied, 'We were traders in the time of Allah's Messenger (ﷺ) and I asked Allah's Messenger (ﷺ) about money exchange. He replied, 'If it is from hand to hand, there is no harm in it; otherwise, it is not permissible." [Al-Bukhari, Book 34, Hadith 14]

Selling of gold for silver from hand to hand

حَدَّثَنَا عِمْرَانُ بْنُ مَيْسَرَةَ، حَدَّثَنَا عَبَّادُ بْنُ الْعَوَّامِ، أَخْبَرَنَا يَحْيَى بْنُ أَبِي إِسْحَاقَ، حَدَّثَنَا عَبْدُ الرَّحْمَنِ بْنُ أَبِي بَكْرَةَ، عَنْ أَبِيهِ ـ رضى الله عنه ـ قَالَ نَهَى النَّبِيُّ صلى الله عليه وسلم عَنِ الْفِضَّةِ بِالْفِضَّةِ وَالذَّهَبِ بِالذَّهَبِ، إِلاَّ سَوَاءً بِسَوَاءٍ، وَأَمَرَنَا أَنْ نَبْتَاعَ الذَّهَبَ بِالْفِضَّةِ كَيْفَ شِئْنَا، وَالْفِضَّةَ بِالذَّهَبِ كَيْفَ شِئْنَا.

21-Narrated `Abdur-Rahman bin Abu Bakra:

that his father said, "The Prophet (ﷺ) forbade the selling of gold for gold and silver for silver except if they are equivalent in weight, and allowed us to sell gold for silver and vice versa as we wished." [Al-Bukhari, Book 34, Hadith 130]

Al-muzabana, al-araya

حَدَّثَنَا يَحْيَى بْنُ بُكَيْرٍ، حَدَّثَنَا اللَّيْثُ، عَنْ عُقَيْلٍ، عَنِ ابْنِ شِهَابٍ، أَخْبَرَنِي سَالِمُ بْنُ عَبْدِ اللَّهِ، عَنْ عَبْدِ اللَّهِ بْنِ عُمَرَ ـ رضى الله عنهما ـ أَنَّ رَسُولَ اللَّهِ صلى الله عليه وسلم قَالَ " لاَ تَبِيعُوا الثَّمَرَ حَتَّى يَبْدُوَ صَلاَحُهُ، وَلاَ تَبِيعُوا الثَّمَرَ بِالتَّمْرِ " قَالَ سَالِمٌ وَأَخْبَرَنِي عَبْدُ اللَّهِ، عَنْ زَيْدِ بْنِ ثَابِتٍ، أَنَّ رَسُولَ اللَّهِ صلى الله عليه وسلم رَخَّصَ بَعْدَ ذَلِكَ فِي بَيْعِ الْعَرِيَّةِ بِالرُّطَبِ أَوْ بِالتَّمْرِ، وَلَمْ يُرَخِّصْ فِي غَيْرِهِ.

22-Narrated `Abdullah bin `Umar:

Allah's Messenger (ﷺ) said, "Do not sell fruits of dates until they become free from all the dangers of being spoilt or blighted; and do not sell fresh dates for dry dates." Narrated Salim and `Abdullah from Zaid bin Thabit' <u>"Later on Allah's Messenger (ﷺ) permitted the selling of ripe fruits on trees for fresh dates or dried dates in Bai'-al-'Araya, and did not allow it for any other kind of sale."</u> [Al-Bukhari, Book 34, Hadith 131]

حَدَّثَنَا عَبْدُ اللَّهِ بْنُ يُوسُفَ، أَخْبَرَنَا مَالِكٌ، عَنْ نَافِعٍ، عَنْ عَبْدِ اللَّهِ بْنِ عُمَرَ ـ رضى الله عنهما ـ أَنَّ رَسُولَ اللَّهِ صلى الله عليه وسلم نَهَى عَنِ الْمُزَابَنَةِ. وَالْمُزَابَنَةُ اشْتِرَاءُ الثَّمَرِ بِالتَّمْرِ كَيْلاً، وَبَيْعُ الْكَرْمِ بِالزَّبِيبِ كَيْلاً.

23-Narrated Abu Sa`id Al-Khudri:

Allah's Messenger (ﷺ) forbade Muzabana and Muhaqala, and Muzabana means the selling of ripe dates for dates still on the trees. [Al-Bukhari, Book 34, Hadith 133]

H-SELLING OF MIXED DATES (A KIND OF USURY)

حَدَّثَنَا أَبُو نُعَيْمٍ، حَدَّثَنَا شَيْبَانُ، عَنْ يَحْيَى، عَنْ أَبِي سَلَمَةَ، عَنْ أَبِي سَعِيدٍ ـ رضى الله عنه ـ قَالَ كُنَّا نُرْزَقُ تَمْرَ الْجَمْعِ، وَهُوَ الْخِلْطُ مِنَ التَّمْرِ، وَكُنَّا نَبِيعُ صَاعَيْنِ بِصَاعٍ فَقَالَ النَّبِيُّ صلى الله عليه وسلم " لاَ صَاعَيْنِ بِصَاعٍ، وَلاَ

دِرْهَمَيْنِ بِدِرْهَمٍ ".

24-Narrated Abu Sa`id:

We used to be given mixed dates (from the booty) and used to sell (barter) two Sas of those dates) for one Sa (of good dates). The Prophet (ﷺ) said (to us), <u>"No (bartering of) two Sas for one Sa nor two Dirhams for one Dirham is permissible", (as that is a kind of usury)</u>. [Al-Bukhari, Book 34, Hadith 33]

Buy dates for riba-al-fadl.

حَدَّثَنَا قُتَيْبَةُ، عَنْ مَالِكٍ، عَنْ عَبْدِ الْمَجِيدِ بْنِ سُهَيْلِ بْنِ عَبْدِ الرَّحْمَنِ، عَنْ سَعِيدِ بْنِ الْمُسَيَّبِ، عَنْ أَبِي سَعِيدٍ الْخُدْرِيِّ، وَعَنْ أَبِي هُرَيْرَةَ ـ رضى الله عنهما ـ أَنَّ رَسُولَ اللَّهِ صلى الله عليه وسلم اسْتَعْمَلَ رَجُلاً عَلَى خَيْبَرَ، فَجَاءَهُ بِتَمْرٍ جَنِيبٍ، فَقَالَ رَسُولُ اللَّهِ صلى الله عليه وسلم " أَكُلُّ تَمْرِ خَيْبَرَ هَكَذَا ". قَالَ لاَ وَاللَّهِ يَا رَسُولَ اللَّهِ، إِنَّا لَنَأْخُذُ الصَّاعَ مِنْ هَذَا بِالصَّاعَيْنِ، وَالصَّاعَيْنِ بِالثَّلاَثَةِ. فَقَالَ رَسُولُ اللَّهِ صلى الله عليه وسلم " لاَ تَفْعَلْ، بِعِ الْجَمْعَ بِالدَّرَاهِمِ، ثُمَّ ابْتَعْ بِالدَّرَاهِمِ جَنِيبًا ".

8-Narrated Abu Sa`id Al-Khudri and Abu Huraira:

Allah's Messenger (ﷺ) appointed somebody as a governor of Khaibar. That governor brought him an excellent kind of dates (from Khaibar). The Prophet (ﷺ) asked, "Are all the dates of Khaibar like this?" He replied, "By Allah, no, O Allah's Messenger (ﷺ)!

But we barter one Sa of this (a type of dates) for two Sas of dates of ours and two Sas of it for three of ours." Allah's Messenger (ﷺ) said, "Do not do so (as that is a kind of usury) but sell the mixed dates (of inferior quality) for money, and then buy good dates with that money." Al-Bukhari, [Book 34, Hadith 148]

I-DISCLOSING DEFECTS

حَدَّثَنَا بَدَلُ بْنُ الْمُحَبَّرِ، حَدَّثَنَا شُعْبَةُ، عَنْ قَتَادَةَ، قَالَ سَمِعْتُ أَبَا الْخَلِيلِ، يُحَدِّثُ عَنْ عَبْدِ اللَّهِ بْنِ الْحَارِثِ، عَنْ حَكِيمِ بْنِ حِزَامٍ، عَنِ النَّبِيِّ صلى الله عليه وسلم قَالَ " الْبَيِّعَانِ بِالْخِيَارِ مَا لَمْ يَتَفَرَّقَا ـ أَوْ قَالَ حَتَّى يَتَفَرَّقَا ـ فَإِنْ صَدَقَا وَبَيَّنَا بُورِكَ لَهُمَا فِي بَيْعِهِمَا، وَإِنْ كَتَمَا وَكَذَبَا مُحِقَتْ بَرَكَةُ بَيْعِهِمَا ".

25-Narrated Hakim bin Hizam:

The Prophet (ﷺ) aid, "The buyer and the seller have the option to cancel or to confirm the deal, as long as they have not parted or till they part, and if they spoke the truth and told each other the defects of the things, then blessings would be in their deal, and if they hid something and told lies, the blessing of the deal would be lost." [Al-Bukhari, Book 34, Hadith 35]

حَدَّثَنَا سُلَيْمَانُ بْنُ حَرْبٍ، حَدَّثَنَا شُعْبَةُ، عَنْ قَتَادَةَ، عَنْ صَالِحٍ أَبِي الْخَلِيلِ، عَنْ عَبْدِ اللَّهِ بْنِ الْحَارِثِ، رَفَعَهُ إِلَى حَكِيمِ بْنِ حِزَامٍ ـ رضى الله عنه ـ قَالَ قَالَ رَسُولُ اللَّهِ صلى الله عليه وسلم " الْبَيِّعَانِ بِالْخِيَارِ مَا لَمْ يَتَفَرَّقَا ـ أَوْ قَالَ حَتَّى يَتَفَرَّقَا ـ

." فَإِنْ صَدَقَا وَبَيَّنَا بُورِكَ لَهُمَا فِي بَيْعِهِمَا، وَإِنْ كَتَمَا وَكَذَبَا مُحِقَتْ بَرَكَةُ بَيْعِهِمَا"

26-Narrated Hakim bin Hizam:

Allah's Messenger (ﷺ) said, "The seller and the buyer have the right to keep or return goods as long as they have not parted or till they part; and if both the <u>parties spoke the truth and described the defects and qualities (of the goods), then they would be blessed in their transaction</u>, and if they told lies or hid something, then the blessings of their transaction would be lost." [Book 34, Hadith 32]

J- SILK IS UNDESIRABLE TO WEAR BUT ALLOWED TO SELL

حَدَّثَنَا آدَمُ، حَدَّثَنَا شُعْبَةُ، حَدَّثَنَا أَبُو بَكْرِ بْنُ حَفْصٍ، عَنْ سَالِمِ بْنِ عَبْدِ اللَّهِ بْنِ عُمَرَ، عَنْ أَبِيهِ، قَالَ أَرْسَلَ النَّبِيُّ صلى الله عليه وسلم إِلَى عُمَرَ ـ رضى الله عنه ـ بِحُلَّةِ حَرِيرٍ ـ أَوْ سِيرَاءَ ـ فَرَآهَا عَلَيْهِ، فَقَالَ " إِنِّي لَمْ أُرْسِلْ بِهَا إِلَيْكَ لِتَلْبَسَهَا، إِنَّمَا يَلْبَسُهَا مَنْ لاَ خَلاَقَ لَهُ، إِنَّمَا بَعَثْتُ إِلَيْكَ لِتَسْتَمْتِعَ بِهَا ". يَعْنِي تَبِيعُهَا.

27-Narrated `Abdullah bin `Umar:

Once the Prophet (ﷺ) sent Umar a silken two-piece garment to him, and when he saw `Umar wearing it, he said to him, <u>"I have not sent it to you to wear it. It is worn by him who has no share in the Hereafter,</u>

and I have sent it to you so that you could receive help from it (i.e., sell it). [Al-Bukhari, Book 34, Hadith 57]

دَّثَنِي مُحَمَّدُ بْنُ بَشَّارٍ، حَدَّثَنَا غُنْدَرٌ، حَدَّثَنَا شُعْبَةُ، عَنْ قَتَادَةَ، عَنِ النَّضْرِ بْنِ أَنَسٍ، عَنْ بَشِيرِ بْنِ نَهِيكٍ، عَنْ أَبِي هُرَيْرَةَ ـ رضى الله عنه ـ عَنِ النَّبِيِّ صلى الله عليه وسلم أَنَّهُ نَهَى عَنْ خَاتَمِ الذَّهَبِ. وَقَالَ عَمْرٌو أَخْبَرَنَا شُعْبَةُ عَنْ قَتَادَةَ سَمِعَ النَّضْرَ سَمِعَ بَشِيرًا مِثْلَهُ.

28-Narrated Abu Huraira:

The Prophet (ﷺ) forbade the wearing of a gold ring. [Al-Bukhari, Book 77, Hadith 81]

K-ARAYA

حَدَّثَنَا مُحَمَّدٌ، أَخْبَرَنَا عَبْدُ اللَّهِ، أَخْبَرَنَا مُوسَى بْنُ عُقْبَةَ، عَنْ نَافِعٍ، عَنِ ابْنِ عُمَرَ، عَنْ زَيْدِ بْنِ ثَابِتٍ ـ رضى الله عنهم ـ أَنَّ رَسُولَ اللَّهِ صلى الله عليه وسلم رَخَّصَ فِي الْعَرَايَا أَنْ تُبَاعَ بِخَرْصِهَا كَيْلاً. قَالَ مُوسَى بْنُ عُقْبَةَ وَالْعَرَايَا نَخَلاَتٌ مَعْلُومَاتٌ تَأْتِيهَا فَتَشْتَرِيهَا.

29-Narrated Ibn `Umar from Zaid bin Thabit:

Allah's Messenger (ﷺ) allowed the sale of 'Araya by estimating the dates on them for measured amounts of dried dates. Musa bin `Uqba said, "Al- 'Araya were distinguished date palms; one could buy them (i.e., their fruits). [Al-Bukhari, Book 34, Hadith 139/2192]

حَدَّثَنَا يَحْيَى بْنُ سُلَيْمَانَ، حَدَّثَنَا ابْنُ وَهْبٍ، أَخْبَرَنَا ابْنُ جُرَيْجٍ، عَنْ عَطَاءٍ، وَأَبِي الزُّبَيْرِ، عَنْ جَابِرٍ ـ رضى الله عنه ـ قَالَ نَهَى النَّبِيُّ صلى الله عليه وسلم عَنْ بَيْعِ الثَّمَرِ حَتَّى يَطِيبَ، وَلاَ يُبَاعُ شَىْءٌ مِنْهُ إِلاَّ بِالدِّينَارِ وَالدِّرْهَمِ إِلاَّ الْعَرَايَا.

30-Narrated Jabir:

The Prophet (ﷺ) <u>forbade the selling of fruits unless they get ripe</u>, and <u>none of them should be sold except for Dinar or Dirham</u> (i.e. money), <u>except the 'Araya trees (the dates of which could be sold for dates)</u>. [Al-Bukhari, Book 34, Hadith 136/2189]

حَدَّثَنَا عَبْدُ اللَّهِ بْنُ عَبْدِ الْوَهَّابِ، قَالَ سَمِعْتُ مَالِكًا، وَسَأَلَهُ، عُبَيْدُ اللَّهِ بْنُ الرَّبِيعِ أَحَدَّثَكَ دَاوُدُ عَنْ أَبِي سُفْيَانَ، عَنْ أَبِي هُرَيْرَةَ ـ رضى الله عنه ـ أَنَّ النَّبِيَّ صلى الله عليه وسلم رَخَّصَ فِي بَيْعِ الْعَرَايَا فِي خَمْسَةِ أَوْسُقٍ أَوْ دُونَ خَمْسَةِ أَوْسُقٍ قَالَ نَعَمْ.

31-Narrated Abu Huraira:

<u>The Prophet (ﷺ) allowed the sale of the dates of 'Araya provided they were about five Awsuq (singular: Wasaq which means sixty Sa's) or less (in amount)</u>. [Al-Bukhari, Book 34, Hadith 137/2190]

حَدَّثَنَا عَلِيُّ بْنُ عَبْدِ اللَّهِ، حَدَّثَنَا سُفْيَانُ، قَالَ قَالَ يَحْيَى بْنُ سَعِيدٍ سَمِعْتُ بُشَيْرًا، قَالَ سَمِعْتُ سَهْلَ بْنَ أَبِي حَثْمَةَ، أَنَّ رَسُولَ اللَّهِ صلى الله عليه وسلم نَهَى عَنْ بَيْعِ الثَّمَرِ بِالتَّمْرِ، وَرَخَّصَ فِي الْعَرِيَّةِ أَنْ تُبَاعَ بِخَرْصِهَا يَأْكُلُهَا أَهْلُهَا رُطَبًا. وَقَالَ سُفْيَانُ مَرَّةً أُخْرَى إِلاَّ أَنَّهُ رَخَّصَ فِي الْعَرِيَّةِ يَبِيعُهَا أَهْلُهَا بِخَرْصِهَا، يَأْكُلُونَهَا رُطَبًا. قَالَ هُوَ سَوَاءٌ. قَالَ سُفْيَانُ فَقُلْتُ لِيَحْيَى وَأَنَا غُلاَمٌ إِنَّ أَهْلَ مَكَّةَ

يَقُولُونَ إِنَّ النَّبِيَّ صلى الله عليه وسلم رَخَّصَ فِي بَيْعِ الْعَرَايَا. فَقَالَ وَمَا يُدْرِي أَهْلَ مَكَّةَ قُلْتُ إِنَّهُمْ يَرْوُونَهُ عَنْ جَابِرٍ. فَسَكَتَ. قَالَ سُفْيَانُ إِنَّمَا أَرَدْتُ أَنَّ جَابِرًا مِنْ أَهْلِ الْمَدِينَةِ. قِيلَ لِسُفْيَانَ وَلَيْسَ فِيهِ نَهْيٌ عَنْ بَيْعِ الثَّمَرِ حَتَّى يَبْدُوَ صَلَاحُهُ قَالَ لَا.

32-Narrated Sahl bin Abu Hathma:

Allah's Messenger (ﷺ) forbade the selling of fruits (fresh dates) for dried dates <u>but allowed the sale of fruits on the 'Araya by estimation and their new owners might eat their dates fresh</u>. Sufyan (in another narration) said, "I told Yahya (a sub-narrator) when I was a mere boy, 'Meccans say that the Prophet (ﷺ) allowed them the sale of the fruits on 'Araya by estimation.' Yahya asked, 'How do the Meccans know about it?' I replied, 'They narrated it (from the Prophet (ﷺ)) through Jabir.' On that, Yahya kept quiet." Sufyan said, "I meant that Jabir belonged to Medina." Sufyan was asked whether in Jabir's narration there any prohibition from being sold fruits before their benefit is clear (i.e., no dangers of being spoilt or blighted). He replied that there was none. [Al-Bukhari, Book 34, Hadith 138/2191]

حَدَّثَنَا عَبْدُ اللَّهِ بْنُ مَسْلَمَةَ، حَدَّثَنَا مَالِكٌ، عَنْ نَافِعٍ، عَنِ ابْنِ عُمَرَ، عَنْ زَيْدِ بْنِ ثَابِتٍ ـ رضى الله عنهم ـ أَنَّ رَسُولَ اللَّهِ صلى الله عليه وسلم أَرْخَصَ لِصَاحِبِ الْعَرِيَّةِ أَنْ يَبِيعَهَا بِخَرْصِهَا.

33-Narrated Zaid bin Thabit:

Allah's Messenger (ﷺ) allowed the owner of 'Araya to sell the fruits on the trees by estimation. [Al-Bukhari, Book 34, Hadith 135]

5 TERMS OF TRANSACTION

INTRODUCTION

The chapter is strongly associated with the earlier one, but it is separated as another chapter to highlight the terms of trade from the process.

The first condition is not to sell un-milked animals because it shows that the animal is able to produce a lot of milk. Animals are normally milked twice a day, which shows their ability to the quantity of milk they produce once. The price of the animal is thus decided as such. If the animal is left un-milked one or more times, the milk would accumulate. Therefore, when it is milked it gives more than the normal quantity. So, the price is decided accordingly, i.e., the seller can demand a higher price than if it were milked regularly.

If the buyer returns the animal and has taken away the animal and milked it once or more times he must pay at least one Sa of dates. It is the price of milk he has milked and used. The third condition is that the buyer needs to return the animal within three days of the date of purchase.

Secondly, no one can impose any condition (s) outside of sharia. In the contemporary terms, it applies to those products which the law of a country prohibits provided it is not against the Islamic sharia. For instance, selling wine is not allowed in Islamic sharia, so, any law of a country about its validity is not acceptable. It means if the law of a country allows its trade, a Muslim cannot do it because the law of Islam is superior to the law of a country. Thus, the ruling applies to other haram products we have mentioned above etc.

Similarly, it is not allowed to sell fruit still on trees whose benefit is not clear (i.e., free from all the dangers of being spoiled or blighted). The condition is still applicable; there are contrary practices for the purchase of fruits etc. which are invalid from the sharia point of view.

Another condition is imposed on pollinated dates: the seller is not permissible to sell such dates. And if there was no condition in the contract of sale the pollinated dates shall be the responsibility of the seller. The ruling applies to other products, i.e., the faulty of the product goes back to the seller. Such a condition is also imposed on the un-milked animals as mentioned above.

Also, the prophet (ﷺ) forbade the exchange of unharvested fruits for a measured quantity of similar fruit i.e., dates for dates and grapes for grapes for grapes for grapes for grapes for grapes for grapes for grapes for grapes for grapes for grapes for grapes for grapes for grapes for grapes for grapes for grapes for grapes.

If there are no terms between the transacting parties, the tradition of the community may be followed to resolve business issues. The prophet (ﷺ) has left some matters unchanged which were prevalent in the pre-prophethood period. Similarly, there was a peace treaty between the tribes of Makkah known as Helf-al-fazool. The prophet (the prophet(used to say that if such a treaty were to be made again, he would be happy to join it.

A town dweller cannot sell on behalf of a desert dweller. It may be due to the lake of information on the part of a desert dweller. The town dweller knows the market price while the desert dweller does not. It means the former can exploit the latter. [Allah knows better]

The time limit has been imposed for a transaction. Under normal circumstances, a transaction is valid when the parties separate from each other. It implies that before separation the transaction can be cancelled. However, the parties involved can stipulate terms of trade as they wish.

Finally, the joint owner of a property has the right of preemption; one hadith is also applicable for any property i.e., preemption is allowed for every property. It is exempted "if the boundaries were well marked or the ways and streets were fixed, then there was no pre-emption."

The chapter consists of nine sub-sections and eighteen ahadith.

A-SELLING AND UN-MILKED ANIMAL

حَدَّثَنَا مُحَمَّدُ بْنُ عَمْرٍو، حَدَّثَنَا الْمَكِّيُّ، أَخْبَرَنَا ابْنُ جُرَيْجٍ، قَالَ أَخْبَرَنِي زِيَادٌ، أَنَّ ثَابِتًا، مَوْلَى عَبْدِ الرَّحْمَنِ بْنِ زَيْدٍ أَخْبَرَهُ أَنَّهُ، سَمِعَ أَبَا هُرَيْرَةَ ـ رضى الله عنه ـ يَقُولُ قَالَ رَسُولُ اللهِ صلى الله عليه وسلم " مَنِ اشْتَرَى غَنَمًا مُصَرَّاةً

فَاحْتَلَبَهَا، فَإِنْ رَضِيَهَا أَمْسَكَهَا، وَإِنْ سَخِطَهَا فَفِي حَلْبَتِهَا صَاعٌ مِنْ تَمْرٍ ".

1-Narrated Abu Huraira:

Allah's Messenger (ﷺ) said, "Whoever buys a sheep which has been kept un-milked for a long period, and milks it, can keep it if he is satisfied, and if he is not satisfied, he can return it, but he should pay one Sa of dates for the milk." [Al-Bukhari, Book 34, Hadith 103]

2-Narrated Abu Huraira:

حَدَّثَنَا ابْنُ بُكَيْرٍ، حَدَّثَنَا اللَّيْثُ، عَنْ جَعْفَرِ بْنِ رَبِيعَةَ، عَنِ الأَعْرَجِ، قَالَ أَبُو هُرَيْرَةَ ـ رضى الله عنه ـ عَنِ النَّبِيِّ صلى الله عليه وسلم " لاَ تُصَرُّوا الإِبِلَ وَالْغَنَمَ، فَمَنِ ابْتَاعَهَا بَعْدُ فَإِنَّهُ بِخَيْرِ النَّظَرَيْنِ بَعْدَ أَنْ يَحْتَلِبَهَا إِنْ شَاءَ أَمْسَكَ، وَإِنْ شَاءَ رَدَّهَا وَصَاعَ تَمْرٍ ". وَيُذْكَرُ عَنْ أَبِي صَالِحٍ وَمُجَاهِدٍ وَالْوَلِيدِ بْنِ رَبَاحٍ وَمُوسَى بْنِ يَسَارٍ عَنْ أَبِي هُرَيْرَةَ عَنِ النَّبِيِّ صلى الله عليه وسلم " صَاعَ تَمْرٍ ". وَقَالَ بَعْضُهُمْ عَنِ ابْنِ سِيرِينَ صَاعًا مِنْ طَعَامٍ وَهُوَ بِالْخِيَارِ ثَلاَثًا. وَقَالَ بَعْضُهُمْ عَنِ ابْنِ سِيرِينَ صَاعًا مِنْ تَمْرٍ. وَلَمْ يَذْكُرْ ثَلاَثًا، وَالتَّمْرُ أَكْثَرُ.

The Prophet (ﷺ) said, "Don't keep camels and sheep un-milked for a long time, for whoever buys such an animal has the option to milk it and then either keep it or return it to the owner along with one Sa of dates." Some narrated from Ibn Seereen (that the Prophet (ﷺ) had said), "One Sa of wheat, and he has the option for three days." And some narrated from Ibn Seereen, " ... a Sa of dates," not mentioning the option for three days. But a Sa of dates is mentioned in most narrations. [Al-Bukhari, Book 34, Hadith 100]

B-IMPOSING UNLAWFUL (NOT ALLOWED IN ISLAM) CONDITIONS

حَدَّثَنَا أَبُو الْيَمَانِ، أَخْبَرَنَا شُعَيْبٌ، عَنِ الزُّهْرِيِّ، قَالَ عُرْوَةُ بْنُ الزُّبَيْرِ قَالَتْ عَائِشَةُ ـ رضى الله عنها دَخَلَ عَلَىَّ رَسُولُ اللَّهِ صلى الله عليه وسلم فَذَكَرْتُ لَهُ، فَقَالَ رَسُولُ اللَّهِ صلى الله عليه وسلم " اشْتَرِي وَأَعْتِقِي، فَإِنَّ الْوَلاَءَ لِمَنْ أَعْتَقَ ". ثُمَّ قَامَ النَّبِيُّ صلى الله عليه وسلم مِنَ الْعَشِيِّ، فَأَثْنَى عَلَى اللَّهِ بِمَا هُوَ أَهْلُهُ، ثُمَّ قَالَ " مَا بَالُ أُنَاسٍ يَشْتَرِطُونَ شُرُوطًا لَيْسَ فِي كِتَابِ اللَّهِ، مَنِ اشْتَرَطَ شَرْطًا لَيْسَ فِي كِتَابِ اللَّهِ فَهْوَ بَاطِلٌ، وَإِنِ اشْتَرَطَ مِائَةَ شَرْطٍ، شَرْطُ اللَّهِ أَحَقُّ وَأَوْثَقُ ".

3-Narrated `Aisha:

Allah's Messenger (ﷺ) came to me and I told him about the slave-girl (Buraira) Allah's Messenger (ﷺ) said, "Buy and manumit [release from slavery] her, for the Wala is for the one who manumits." In the evening, the Prophet (ﷺ) got up and glorified Allah as He deserved and then said, "Why do some people impose conditions which are not present in Allah's Book (Laws)? Whoever imposes such a condition as is not in Allah's Laws, then that condition is invalid even if he imposes one hundred conditions, for Allah's conditions, are more binding and dependable." [Al-Bukhari, Book 34, Hadith

C-THE SALE OF FRUITS BEFORE THEIR BENEFIT IS EVIDENT

وَقَالَ اللَّيْثُ عَنْ أَبِي الزِّنَادِ، كَانَ عُرْوَةُ بْنُ الزُّبَيْرِ يُحَدِّثُ عَنْ سَهْلِ بْنِ أَبِي حَثْمَةَ الْأَنْصَارِيِّ، مِنْ بَنِي حَارِثَةَ أَنَّهُ حَدَّثَهُ عَنْ زَيْدِ بْنِ ثَابِتٍ ـ رضى الله عنه ـ قَالَ كَانَ النَّاسُ فِي عَهْدِ رَسُولِ اللَّهِ صلى الله عليه وسلم يَتَبَايَعُونَ الثِّمَارَ، فَإِذَا جَدَّ النَّاسُ وَحَضَرَ تَقَاضِيهِمْ قَالَ الْمُبْتَاعُ إِنَّهُ أَصَابَ الثَّمَرَ الدَّمَانُ أَصَابَهُ مُرَاضٌ أَصَابَهُ قُشَامٌ ـ عَاهَاتٌ يَحْتَجُّونَ بِهَا ـ فَقَالَ رَسُولُ اللَّهِ صلى الله عليه وسلم لَمَّا كَثُرَتْ عِنْدَهُ الْخُصُومَةُ فِي ذَلِكَ " فَإِمَّا لاَ فَلاَ يَتَبَايَعُوا حَتَّى يَبْدُوَ صَلاَحُ الثَّمَرِ ". كَالْمَشُورَةِ يُشِيرُ بِهَا لِكَثْرَةِ خُصُومَتِهِمْ. وَأَخْبَرَنِي خَارِجَةُ بْنُ زَيْدِ بْنِ ثَابِتٍ أَنَّ زَيْدَ بْنَ ثَابِتٍ لَمْ يَكُنْ يَبِيعُ ثِمَارَ أَرْضِهِ حَتَّى تَطْلُعَ الثُّرَيَّا فَيَتَبَيَّنَ الْأَصْفَرُ مِنَ الْأَحْمَرِ.

قَالَ أَبُو عَبْدِ اللَّهِ رَوَاهُ عَلِيُّ بْنُ بَحْرٍ حَدَّثَنَا حَكَّامٌ حَدَّثَنَا عَنْبَسَةُ عَنْ زَكَرِيَّاءَ عَنْ أَبِي الزِّنَادِ عَنْ عُرْوَةَ عَنْ سَهْلٍ عَنْ زَيْدٍ

4-Zaid bin Thabit (RA) said,

"In the lifetime of Allah's Messenger (ﷺ), the people used to trade with fruits. When they cut their date-fruits and the purchasers came to receive their rights, the seller would say, 'My dates have got rotten, they are blighted with the disease, they are afflicted with Qusham (a disease which causes the fruit to fall before ripening).' They would go on complaining about defects in their purchases. Allah's Messenger (ﷺ) said, "<u>Do not sell the fruits before their benefit is evident</u> (i.e. free from all the dangers of being spoiled or blighted), by way of advice for they quarreled too much." Kharija bin Zaid bin Thabit said that Zaid bin Thabit (RA) used not to sell the fruits of his land till the Pleiades appeared and one could distinguish the yellow fruits from the red (ripe) ones. [Al-Bukhari, Book 34, Hadith 140]

حَدَّثَنَا ابْنُ مُقَاتِلٍ، أَخْبَرَنَا عَبْدُ اللَّهِ، أَخْبَرَنَا حُمَيْدٌ الطَّوِيلُ، عَنْ أَنَسٍ ـ رضى الله عنه ـ أَنَّ رَسُولَ اللَّهِ صلى الله عليه وسلم نَهَى أَنْ تُبَاعَ ثَمَرَةُ النَّخْلِ حَتَّى تَزْهُوَ‏.‏ قَالَ أَبُو عَبْدِ اللَّهِ يَعْنِي حَتَّى تَحْمَرَّ‏.‏

5-Narrated Anas:

Allah's Messenger (ﷺ) forbade the sale of date fruits till they were ripe. Abu `Abdullah (Al-Bukhari) said, "That means till they were red" (can be eaten). [Al-Bukhari, Book 34, Hadith 142]

حَدَّثَنَا عَبْدُ اللَّهِ بْنُ يُوسُفَ، أَخْبَرَنَا مَالِكٌ، عَنْ نَافِعٍ، عَنْ عَبْدِ اللَّهِ بْنِ عُمَرَ ـ رضى الله عنهما ـ أَنَّ رَسُولَ اللَّهِ صلى الله عليه وسلم نَهَى عَنْ بَيْعِ الثِّمَارِ حَتَّى يَبْدُوَ صَلاَحُهَا، نَهَى الْبَائِعَ وَالْمُبْتَاعَ‏.‏

6-Narrated `Abdullah bin `Umar:

Allah's Messenger (ﷺ) forbade the sale of fruits till their benefit is clear. He forbade both the seller and the buyer (such sale). [Al-Bukhari, Book 34, Hadith 141]

حَدَّثَنَا عَبْدُ اللهِ بْنُ يُوسُفَ، أَخْبَرَنَا مَالِكٌ، عَنْ حُمَيْدٍ، عَنْ أَنَسِ بْنِ مَالِكٍ ـ رضى الله عنه ـ أَنَّ رَسُولَ اللهِ صلى الله عليه وسلم نَهَى عَنْ بَيْعِ الثِّمَارِ حَتَّى تُزْهِيَ. فَقِيلَ لَهُ وَمَا تُزْهِي قَالَ حَتَّى تَحْمَرَّ. فَقَالَ " أَرَأَيْتَ إِذَا مَنَعَ اللهُ الثَّمَرَةَ، بِمَ يَأْخُذُ أَحَدُكُمْ مَالَ أَخِيهِ ".

7-Narrated Anas bin Malik:

Allah's Messenger (ﷺ) forbade the sale of fruits till they are almost ripe. He was asked what is meant by 'are almost ripe.' He replied, "Till they become red." Allah's Messenger (ﷺ) further said, <u>"If Allah spoiled the fruits, what right would one have to take the money of one's brother (i.e. other people)?"</u> [Al-Bukhari, Book 34, Hadith 145]

قَالَ اللَّيْثُ حَدَّثَنِي يُونُسُ، عَنِ ابْنِ شِهَابٍ، قَالَ لَوْ أَنَّ رَجُلاً، ابْتَاعَ ثَمَرًا قَبْلَ أَنْ يَبْدُوَ صَلاَحُهُ، ثُمَّ أَصَابَتْهُ عَاهَةٌ، كَانَ مَا أَصَابَهُ عَلَى رَبِّهِ، أَخْبَرَنِي سَالِمُ بْنُ عَبْدِ اللَّهِ عَنِ ابْنِ عُمَرَ ـ رضى الله عنهما ـ أَنَّ رَسُولَ اللهِ صلى الله عليه وسلم قَالَ " لاَ تَتَبَايَعُوا الثَّمَرَ حَتَّى يَبْدُوَ صَلاَحُهَا، وَلاَ تَبِيعُوا الثَّمَرَ بِالتَّمْرِ ".

8-Narrated Ibn Shihab:

If somebody bought fruit before their benefit is clear and then the fruits were spoiled with blights, the loss would be suffered by the owner (not the buyer).

Narrated Salim bin 'Abdullah from Ibn Umar: Allah's Messenger (ﷺ) said, "Do not sell or buy fruits before their benefit was evident and do not sell fresh fruits (dates) for dried dates." [Al-Bukhari, Book 34, Hadith 146]

D- POLLINATED DATES

قَالَ أَبُو عَبْدِ اللهِ وَقَالَ لِي إِبْرَاهِيمُ أَخْبَرَنَا هِشَامٌ، أَخْبَرَنَا ابْنُ جُرَيْجٍ، قَالَ سَمِعْتُ ابْنَ أَبِي مُلَيْكَةَ، يُخْبِرُ عَنْ نَافِعٍ، مَوْلَى ابْنِ عُمَرَ أَنَّ أَيُّمَا، نَخْلٍ بِيعَتْ قَدْ أُبِّرَتْ لَمْ يُذْكَرِ الثَّمَرُ، فَالثَّمَرُ لِلَّذِي أَبَرَهَا، وَكَذَلِكَ الْعَبْدُ وَالْحَرْثُ. سَمَّى لَهُ نَافِعٌ هَؤُلَاءِ الثَّلَاثَ.

9-Narrated Nafi', the freed slave of Ibn 'Umar:

<u>If pollinated date-palms are sold and nothing is mentioned (in the contract) about their fruits, the fruits will go to the person who has pollinated them,</u> and so will be the case with the slave and the cultivator. Nafi' mentioned those three things. [Al-Bukhari, Book 34, Hadith 149]

حَدَّثَنَا عَبْدُ اللهِ بْنُ يُوسُفَ، أَخْبَرَنَا مَالِكٌ، عَنْ نَافِعٍ، عَنْ عَبْدِ اللهِ بْنِ عُمَرَ ـ رضى الله عنهما ـ أَنَّ رَسُولَ اللهِ صلى الله عليه وسلم قَالَ " مَنْ بَاعَ نَخْلًا قَدْ أُبِّرَتْ فَثَمَرُهَا لِلْبَائِعِ، إِلَّا أَنْ يَشْتَرِطَ الْمُبْتَاعُ ".

10-Narrated `Abdullah bin `Umar:

Allah's Messenger (ﷺ) said, "<u>If somebody sells pollinated date palms, the fruits will be for the seller unless the buyer stipulates that they will be</u>

for himself (and the seller agrees). [Al-Bukhari, Book 34, Hadith 150]

E-THE SALE OF UNHARVESTED CROPS FOR A MEASURED QUANTITY OF FOODSTUFF

حَدَّثَنَا قُتَيْبَةُ، حَدَّثَنَا اللَّيْثُ، عَنْ نَافِعٍ، عَنِ ابْنِ عُمَرَ ـ رضى الله عنهما ـ قَالَ نَهَى رَسُولُ اللَّهِ صلى الله عليه وسلم عَنِ الْمُزَابَنَةِ أَنْ يَبِيعَ ثَمَرَ حَائِطِهِ إِنْ كَانَ نَخْلاً بِتَمْرٍ كَيْلاً، وَإِنْ كَانَ كَرْمًا أَنْ يَبِيعَهُ بِزَبِيبٍ كَيْلاً أَوْ كَانَ زَرْعًا أَنْ يَبِيعَهُ بِكَيْلِ طَعَامٍ، وَنَهَى عَنْ ذَلِكَ كُلِّهِ.

11-Narrated Ibn `Umar:

Allah's Messenger (ﷺ) forbade Al-Muzabana, i.e. to sell <u>un-gathered dates of one's garden for measured dried dates or fresh un-gathered grapes for measured dried grapes, or standing crops for the measured quantity of foodstuff</u>. He forbade all such bargains. [Al-Bukhari, Book 34, Hadith 151]

F-NO FIXED JUDGEMENT

وَقَالَ شُرَيْحٌ لِلْغَزَّالِينَ سُنَّتُكُمْ بَيْنَكُمْ رِبْحًا

وَقَالَ عَبْدُ الْوَهَّابِ عَنْ أَيُّوبَ عَنْ مُحَمَّدٍ لاَ بَأْسَ الْعَشَرَةُ بِأَحَدَ عَشَرَ، وَيَأْخُذُ لِلنَّفَقَةِ رِبْحًا.

وَقَالَ النَّبِيُّ صَلَّى اللهُ عَلَيْهِ وَسَلَّمَ لِهِنْدٍ: «خُذِي مَا يَكْفِيكِ وَوَلَدَكِ بِالْمَعْرُوفِ».

وَقَالَ تَعَالَى: {وَمَنْ كَانَ فَقِيرًا فَلْيَأْكُلْ بِالْمَعْرُوفِ} وَاكْتَرَى الْحَسَنُ مِنْ عَبْدِ اللَّهِ بْنِ مِرْدَاسٍ حِمَارًا، فَقَالَ بِكَمْ قَالَ بِدَانَقَيْنِ. فَرَكِبَهُ، ثُمَّ جَاءَ مَرَّةً أُخْرَى، فَقَالَ الْحِمَارَ الْحِمَارَ. فَرَكِبَهُ، وَلَمْ يُشَارِطْهُ، فَبَعَثَ إِلَيْهِ بِنِصْفِ دِرْهَمٍ

12-Shuraih told the weavers,

"You are permitted to follow your own conventions to solve your problems (it is legal for you to stick to your traditions in the bargain). " Narrated `Abdul Wahab: Aiyub said: Muhammad said, "There is no harm in selling for eleven what you buy for ten, and you are allowed to take a profit for expenses. " The Prophet told Hind, "Take what is reasonable and sufficient for you and your sons," Allah says: Whoever is poor, can eat (from the orphan's property) reasonably (according to his labours). <u>Al-Hasan hired a donkey from `Abdullah bin Mirdas and asked him about the hire. The latter replied that it was for two Daniqs (a Daniq equals 116th Dirham). So, Al-Hasan rode away. Another time, Al-Hasan came to `Abdullah bin Mirdas and asked him to hire the donkey for him and rode away without asking him about the hire, but he sent him half a Dirham.</u> [Al-Bukhari, Book 34, Introduction Ch. 95]

G-BROKER

حَدَّثَنَا الصَّلْتُ بْنُ مُحَمَّدٍ، حَدَّثَنَا عَبْدُ الْوَاحِدِ، حَدَّثَنَا مَعْمَرٌ، عَنْ عَبْدِ اللَّهِ بْنِ طَاوُسٍ، عَنْ أَبِيهِ، عَنِ ابْنِ عَبَّاسٍ ـ رضى الله عنهما ـ قَالَ قَالَ رَسُولُ اللَّهِ

صلى الله عليه وسلم " لاَ تَلَقَّوْا الرُّكْبَانَ وَلاَ يَبِيعُ حَاضِرٌ لِبَادٍ ". قَالَ فَقُلْتُ لِابْنِ عَبَّاسٍ مَا قَوْلُهُ لاَ يَبِيعُ حَاضِرٌ لِبَادٍ قَالَ لاَ يَكُونُ لَهُ سِمْسَارًا.

13-Narrated Tawus:

Ibn `Abbas said, "Allah's Messenger (ﷺ) said, 'Do not go to meet the caravans on the way (for buying their goods without letting them know the market price); a town dweller should not sell the goods of a desert dweller on behalf of the latter.' I asked Ibn `Abbas, 'What does he mean by not selling the goods of a desert dweller by a town dweller?' He said, 'He should not become his broker.' " [Al-Bukhari, Book 34, Hadith 109h.

H-TIME LIMIT FOR SALE

حَدَّثَنِي إِسْحَاقُ، أَخْبَرَنَا حَبَّانُ، حَدَّثَنَا شُعْبَةُ، قَالَ قَتَادَةُ أَخْبَرَنِي عَنْ صَالِحٍ أَبِي الْخَلِيلِ، عَنْ عَبْدِ اللَّهِ بْنِ الْحَارِثِ، قَالَ سَمِعْتُ حَكِيمَ بْنَ حِزَامٍ ـ رضى الله عنه ـ عَنِ النَّبِيِّ صلى الله عليه وسلم قَالَ " الْبَيِّعَانِ بِالْخِيَارِ مَا لَمْ يَتَفَرَّقَا، فَإِنْ صَدَقَا وَبَيَّنَا بُورِكَ لَهُمَا فِي بَيْعِهِمَا، وَإِنْ كَذَبَا وَكَتَمَا مُحِقَتْ بَرَكَةُ بَيْعِهِمَا ".

14-Narrated Hakim bin Hizam:

The Prophet (ﷺ) said, "The buyer and the seller have the option of canceling or confirming the bargain unless they separate, and if they spoke the truth and made clear the defects of the goods, them they would be blessed in their bargain, and if they told lies and hid some facts, their bargain would be deprived of Allah's blessings." [Al-Bukhari, Book 34, Hadith 63]

حَدَّثَنَا مُحَمَّدُ بْنُ يُوسُفَ، حَدَّثَنَا سُفْيَانُ، عَنْ عَبْدِ اللَّهِ بْنِ دِينَارٍ، عَنِ ابْنِ عُمَرَ ـ رضى الله عنهما ـ عَنِ النَّبِيِّ صلى الله عليه وسلم قَالَ " كُلُّ بَيِّعَيْنِ لاَ بَيْعَ بَيْنَهُمَا حَتَّى يَتَفَرَّقَا، إِلاَّ بَيْعَ الْخِيَارِ ".

15-Narrated Ibn `Umar:

The Prophet (ﷺ) said, "No deal is settled and finalized unless the buyer and the seller separate, except if the deal is optional" (whereby the validity of the bargain depends on the stipulations agreed upon). [Al-Bukhari, Book 34, Hadith 66]

I-JOINT PROPERTY AS A PRODUCT AND THE RIGHT OF PREEMPTION

عَنِ الزُّهْرِيِّ، عَنْ مَعْمَرٍ، أَخْبَرَنَا الرَّزَّاقِ، عَبْدُ حَدَّثَنَا مَحْمُودٌ، حَدَّثَنِي اللهِ صلى اللَّهِ رَسُولُ جَعَلَ ـ عنه الله رضى جَابِرٍ عَنْ سَلَمَةَ، أَبِي وَصُرِّفَتِ الْحُدُودُ وَقَعَتِ فَإِذَا يُقْسَمْ، لَمْ مَالٍ كُلِّ فِي الشُّفْعَةَ وسلم عليه شُفْعَةَ فَلاَ الطُّرُقُ.

16-Narrated Jabir:

Allah's Messenger (ﷺ) gave preemption (to the

partner) in every joint property, but if the boundaries of the property were demarcated or the ways and streets were fixed, then there was no pre-emption. [Al-Bukhari, Book 34, Hadith 159]

حَدَّثَنَا مُحَمَّدُ بْنُ مَحْبُوبٍ، حَدَّثَنَا عَبْدُ الْوَاحِدِ، حَدَّثَنَا مَعْمَرٌ، عَنِ الزُّهْرِيِّ، عَنْ أَبِي سَلَمَةَ بْنِ عَبْدِ الرَّحْمَنِ، عَنْ جَابِرِ بْنِ عَبْدِ اللَّهِ ـ رضى الله عنهما ـ قَالَ قَضَى النَّبِيُّ صلى الله عليه وسلم بِالشُّفْعَةِ فِي كُلِّ مَالٍ لَمْ يُقْسَمْ، فَإِذَا وَقَعَتِ الْحُدُودُ وَصُرِّفَتِ الطُّرُقُ فَلاَ شُفْعَةَ.

17-Narrated Jabir bin `Abdullah:

Allah's Messenger (ﷺ) decided the validity of preemption in every joint undivided property, but if the boundaries were well marked or the ways and streets were fixed, then there was no pre-emption. [Al-Bukhari, Book 34, Hadith 160]

حَدَّثَنَا مُسَدَّدٌ، حَدَّثَنَا عَبْدُ الْوَاحِدِ، بِهَذَا وَقَالَ فِي كُلِّ مَا لَمْ يُقْسَمْ. تَابَعَهُ هِشَامٌ عَنْ مَعْمَرٍ. قَالَ عَبْدُ الرَّزَّاقِ فِي كُلِّ مَالٍ. رَوَاهُ عَبْدُ الرَّحْمَنِ بْنُ إِسْحَاقَ عَنِ الزُّهْرِيِّ.

18-Narrated Mussaddad from `Abdul Wahid:

the same as above but said, "... in every joint undivided thing..." Narrated Hisham from Ma`mar the same as above but said, " ... in every property... " [Al-Bukhari, Book 34, Hadith 161]

6 PRICE

INTRODUCTION

It is related to three dimensions: payment of the price in advance, purchases made for delayed payment and paying price in cash. The chapter has six ahadith. Marketing texts discuss determination of prices for existing and new products. It is also shown in one of the ahadith included in this collection. It is recommended that the price should be decided justly. It implies a reasonable profit margin should be decided because a Muslim businessperson is receiving the profit and the mercy of Allah. So, the reward is dual. He receives one part of it in this world which is visible and receives the second part in the Hereafter, the invisible one. However, an honest businessperson can perceive the benefits of doing trade for the pleasure of Allah. The pages of history unfolded that Abdurrehman bin Ouff (RA) migrated to Madinah bare handed but became a rich businessperson in a brief period.

A-PAYING IN ADVANCE

حَدَّثَنَا عَمْرُو بْنُ زُرَارَةَ، أَخْبَرَنَا إِسْمَاعِيلُ ابْنُ عُلَيَّةَ، أَخْبَرَنَا ابْنُ أَبِي نَجِيحٍ، عَنْ عَبْدِ اللَّهِ بْنِ كَثِيرٍ، عَنْ أَبِي الْمِنْهَالِ، عَنِ ابْنِ عَبَّاسٍ ـ رضى الله عنهما ـ قَالَ قَدِمَ رَسُولُ اللَّهِ صلى الله عليه وسلم الْمَدِينَةَ، وَالنَّاسُ يُسْلِفُونَ فِي الثَّمَرِ الْعَامَ وَالْعَامَيْنِ ـ أَوْ قَالَ عَامَيْنِ أَوْ ثَلاَثَةً. شَكَّ إِسْمَاعِيلُ ـ فَقَالَ " مَنْ سَلَّفَ فِي تَمْرٍ فَلْيُسْلِفْ فِي كَيْلٍ مَعْلُومٍ، وَوَزْنٍ مَعْلُومٍ ".

1-Narrated Ibn `Abbas,

Allah's Messenger (ﷺ) came to Medina and the people used to pay in advance the price of fruits to be delivered within one or two years. (The sub-narrator is in doubt whether it was one to two years or two to three years.) The Prophet (ﷺ) said, <u>"Whoever pays money in advance for dates (to be delivered later) should pay it for known specified weight and measure (of the dates).</u> [Al-Bukhari, Vol. 3, Book 35, Hadith 441/2239]

حَدَّثَنَا أَبُو الْوَلِيدِ، حَدَّثَنَا شُعْبَةُ، عَنِ ابْنِ أَبِي الْمُجَالِدِ،. وَحَدَّثَنَا يَحْيَى، حَدَّثَنَا وَكِيعٌ، عَنْ شُعْبَةَ، عَنْ مُحَمَّدِ بْنِ أَبِي الْمُجَالِدِ، حَدَّثَنَا حَفْصُ بْنُ عُمَرَ، حَدَّثَنَا شُعْبَةُ، قَالَ أَخْبَرَنِي مُحَمَّدٌ،، أَوْ عَبْدُ اللَّهِ بْنُ أَبِي الْمُجَالِدِ قَالَ اخْتَلَفَ عَبْدُ اللَّهِ بْنُ شَدَّادِ بْنِ الْهَادِ وَأَبُو بُرْدَةَ فِي السَّلَفِ، فَبَعَثُونِي إِلَى ابْنِ أَبِي أَوْفَى ـ رضى الله عنه ـ فَسَأَلْتُهُ فَقَالَ إِنَّا كُنَّا نُسْلِفُ عَلَى عَهْدِ رَسُولِ اللَّهِ صلى الله عليه وسلم

وَأَبِي بَكْرٍ وَعُمَرَ، فِي الْحِنْطَةِ، وَالشَّعِيرِ وَالزَّبِيبِ، وَالتَّمْرِ. وَسَأَلْتُ ابْنَ أَبْزَى فَقَالَ مِثْلَ ذَلِكَ.

2-Narrated Shu`ba,

Muhammad or `Abdullah bin Abu Al-Mujahid said, "Abdullah bin Shaddad and Abu Burda differed regarding As-Salam, so they sent me to Ibn Abi `Aufa and I asked him about it. He replied, 'In the lifetime of Allah's Messenger (ﷺ), Abu Bakr and `Umar, we used to pay in advance the prices of wheat, barley, dried grapes and dates to be delivered later. I also asked Ibn Absa and he, too, replied as above.' " [Al-Bukhari, Vol. 3, Book 35, Hadith 446/2242/2243]

حَدَّثَنَا قُتَيْبَةُ، حَدَّثَنَا سُفْيَانُ، عَنِ ابْنِ أَبِي نَجِيحٍ، عَنْ عَبْدِ اللَّهِ بْنِ كَثِيرٍ، عَنْ أَبِي الْمِنْهَالِ، قَالَ سَمِعْتُ ابْنَ عَبَّاسٍ ـ رضى الله عنهما ـ يَقُولُ قَدِمَ النَّبِيُّ صلى الله عليه وسلم وَقَالَ " فِي كَيْلٍ مَعْلُومٍ وَوَزْنٍ مَعْلُومٍ إِلَى أَجَلٍ مَعْلُومٍ ".

3-Narrated Ibn `Abbas,

The Prophet (ﷺ) came (to Medina) and he told the people (regarding the payment of money in advance that they should pay it) for a known specified measure and a known specified weight <u>and a known</u>

specified period. [Al-Bukhari, Vol. 3, Book 35, Hadith 445/2241]

حَدَّثَنَا بِشْرُ بْنُ مُحَمَّدٍ، أَخْبَرَنَا عَبْدُ اللَّهِ، أَخْبَرَنَا سَعِيدُ بْنُ أَبِي عَرُوبَةَ، عَنْ قَتَادَةَ، عَنِ النَّضْرِ بْنِ أَنَسٍ، عَنْ بَشِيرِ بْنِ نَهِيكٍ، عَنْ أَبِي هُرَيْرَةَ ـ رضى الله عنه ـ عَنِ النَّبِيِّ صلى الله عليه وسلم قَالَ " مَنْ أَعْتَقَ شَقِيصًا مِنْ مَمْلُوكِهِ فَعَلَيْهِ خَلاَصُهُ فِي مَالِهِ، فَإِنْ لَمْ يَكُنْ لَهُ مَالٌ قُوِّمَ الْمَمْلُوكُ، قِيمَةَ عَدْلٍ ثُمَّ اسْتُسْعِيَ غَيْرَ مَشْقُوقٍ عَلَيْهِ ".

4-Narrated Abu Huraira.

The Prophet (ﷺ) said, "Whoever manumits his share of a jointly possessed slave, it is imperative for him to get that slave manumitted completely by paying the remaining price, and if he does not have sufficient money to manumit him, then the price of the slave should be estimated justly, and he is to be allowed to work and earn the amount that will manumit him (without overburdening him)". [Al-Bukhari, Vol. 3, Book 44, Hadith 672/2492]

B-CREDIT PURCHASE

حَدَّثَنِي مُحَمَّدُ بْنُ مَحْبُوبٍ، حَدَّثَنَا عَبْدُ الْوَاحِدِ، حَدَّثَنَا الأَعْمَشُ، قَالَ تَذَاكَرْنَا عِنْدَ إِبْرَاهِيمَ الرَّهْنَ فِي السَّلَفِ فَقَالَ حَدَّثَنِي الأَسْوَدُ عَنْ عَائِشَةَ ـ رضى الله عنها ـ أَنَّ النَّبِيَّ صلى الله عليه وسلم اشْتَرَى مِنْ يَهُودِيٍّ طَعَامًا إِلَى أَجَلٍ مَعْلُومٍ، وَارْتَهَنَ مِنْهُ دِرْعًا مِنْ حَدِيدٍ.

5-Narrated Al-A`mash,

We argued at Ibrahim's dwelling place about mortgaging in Salam. He said, "Aisha said, 'The Prophet (ﷺ) bought some foodstuff from a Jew <u>on credit</u> and the payment was to be made by a definite period, and he mortgaged his iron armor to him." [Al-Bukhari, Vol. 3, Book 35, Hadith 454/2252]

حَدَّثَنَا فَرْوَةُ بْنُ أَبِي الْمَغْرَاءِ، أَخْبَرَنَا عَلِيُّ بْنُ مُسْهِرٍ، عَنْ هِشَامٍ، عَنْ أَبِيهِ، عَنْ عَائِشَةَ ـ رضى الله عنها ـ قَالَتْ لَقَلَّ يَوْمٌ كَانَ يَأْتِي عَلَى النَّبِيِّ صلى الله عليه وسلم إِلاَّ يَأْتِي فِيهِ بَيْتَ أَبِي بَكْرٍ أَحَدَ طَرَفَي النَّهَارِ، فَلَمَّا أُذِنَ لَهُ فِي الْخُرُوجِ إِلَى الْمَدِينَةِ لَمْ يَرُعْنَا إِلاَّ وَقَدْ أَتَانَا ظُهْرًا، فَخُبِّرَ بِهِ أَبُو بَكْرٍ فَقَالَ مَا جَاءَنَا النَّبِيُّ صلى الله عليه وسلم فِي هَذِهِ السَّاعَةِ، إِلاَّ لأَمْرٍ حَدَثَ، فَلَمَّا دَخَلَ عَلَيْهِ قَالَ لأَبِي بَكْرٍ " أَخْرِجْ مَنْ عِنْدَكَ ". قَالَ يَا رَسُولَ اللَّهِ إِنَّمَا هُمَا ابْنَتَاىَ. يَعْنِي عَائِشَةَ وَأَسْمَاءَ. قَالَ " أَشَعَرْتَ أَنَّهُ قَدْ أُذِنَ لِي فِي الْخُرُوجِ ". قَالَ الصُّحْبَةَ يَا رَسُولَ اللَّهِ. قَالَ " الصُّحْبَةَ ". قَالَ يَا رَسُولَ اللَّهِ إِنَّ عِنْدِي نَاقَتَيْنِ أَعْدَدْتُهُمَا لِلْخُرُوجِ، فَخُذْ إِحْدَاهُمَا. قَالَ " قَدْ أَخَذْتُهَا بِالثَّمَنِ ".

6-Narrated Aisha:

Rarely did the Prophet (ﷺ) do not visit Abu Bakr's house every day, either in the morning or in the evening. When the permission for migration to Medina was granted, suddenly, the Prophet (ﷺ)

came to us at noon and Abu Bakr was informed, who said, "Certainly the Prophet (ﷺ) has come for some urgent matter." The Prophet (ﷺ) said to Abu Bakr when the latter entered "Let nobody stay in your home." Abu Bakr said, "O Allah's Messenger (ﷺ)! There are only my two daughters (namely `Aisha and Asma') present." The Prophet (ﷺ) said, "I feel (am informed) that I have been granted permission for migration." Abu Bakr said, "I will accompany you, O Allah's Messenger (ﷺ)!" The Prophet (ﷺ) said, "You will accompany me." Abu Bakr then said "O Allah's Messenger (ﷺ)! I have two she-camels I have prepared specially for migration, so I offer you one of them. The Prophet (ﷺ) said, "I have accepted it on condition that I will pay its price." [Al-Bukhari, book 34, Hadith 90] See same in a credit purchase.

7 PLACE

INTRODUCTION

It is not much about the topic, but basic principles have been articulated for the guidance of business transactions. In the first place, it is recommended to take the products on the market. The emphasis is on the rights of a seller who should receive the right price for his products. People due to human nature try to go outside of the town to receive caravans on the way to Makkah to buy the products cheap. The traders were usually used to bring goods from Syria and Yemen, so they did not know the prevalent price of various products. It was since if two caravans arrived at the town from saying Syria and Yemen; the price due to demand and supply system, were less i.e., the products were cheaper. However, in the case of a single caravan, the prices might be high. It is related to the timing of caravans; if they arrive in succession or on a regular basis then prices were believed to be stable.

As far as storage is concerned, I have not found any details. However, it is known that Abu Bakr (RA) had many shops in Makkah for which he might have some facility. The distribution channels were straight forward as can be decided from the ahadith. The manufacturer or produces were foreigners as mentioned above and the whole seller were the people who used to buy of them and carried the goods in Makkah. The retailers were buying them. It was also possible in case of Abu Bakr (RA) that he might buy goods from Syria and Yemen and sell them on his shops. In this case, the distribution channels would be less than one layer i.e., Produce-wholesaler/retailers. It is because the wholesaler and retailer were one party.

The second matter is related to the place, i.e., possession of goods before they are sold to another party. It suggests the involvement of people in fictitious transactions. It is so because influential traders can buy goods from the market without taking possession and selling them to others. It looks like the trader does not assume any risk or does not make any effort to look after the goods, but he sells them to others without taking goods into possession. Taking it into possession and transporting it to a storage place which was their own homes in those days (but the principle is equally applicable to modern warehouses or store) generates risk. It could be a risk in transportation, change of price, and arrangement of storage, for example. It is universally acceptable that profit is the consequence of investing money (capital) and assuming the risk. Riba is prohibited due to lack of one of these factors, i.e., risk of loss or volatility of profit. Thus, it demands possession of goods before selling to others. The chapter has three sections and nine ahadith.

A- GOING OUT FOR TRADING

دَّثَنَا مُحَمَّدُ بْنُ سَلَامٍ، أَخْبَرَنَا مَخْلَدُ بْنُ يَزِيدَ، أَخْبَرَنَا ابْنُ جُرَيْجٍ، قَالَ أَخْبَرَنِي عَطَاءٌ، عَنْ عُبَيْدِ بْنِ عُمَيْرٍ، أَنَّ أَبَا مُوسَى الْأَشْعَرِيَّ، اسْتَأْذَنَ عَلَى عُمَرَ بْنِ الْخَطَّابِ ـ رضى الله عنه ـ فَلَمْ يُؤْذَنْ لَهُ، وَكَأَنَّهُ كَانَ مَشْغُولاً فَرَجَعَ أَبُو مُوسَى، فَفَرَغَ عُمَرُ فَقَالَ أَلَمْ أَسْمَعْ صَوْتَ عَبْدِ اللَّهِ بْنِ قَيْسٍ انْذَنُوا لَهُ قِيلَ قَدْ رَجَعَ. فَدَعَاهُ. فَقَالَ كُنَّا نُؤْمَرُ بِذَلِكَ. فَقَالَ تَأْتِينِي عَلَى ذَلِكَ بِالْبَيِّنَةِ. فَانْطَلَقَ إِلَى مَجْلِسِ الْأَنْصَارِ، فَسَأَلَهُمْ. فَقَالُوا لاَ يَشْهَدُ لَكَ عَلَى هَذَا إِلاَّ أَصْغَرُنَا أَبُو سَعِيدٍ الْخُدْرِيُّ. فَذَهَبَ بِأَبِي سَعِيدٍ الْخُدْرِيِّ. فَقَالَ عُمَرُ أَخَفِيَ عَلَيَّ مِنْ أَمْرِ رَسُولِ اللَّهِ صلى الله عليه وسلم أَلْهَانِي الصَّفْقُ بِالأَسْوَاقِ. يَعْنِي الْخُرُوجَ إِلَى تِجَارَةٍ.

1-Narrated 'Ubaid bin `Umair:

Abu Musa asked `Umar to admit him but he was not admitted as `Umar was busy, so Abu Musa went back. When `Umar finished his job he said, "Didn't I hear the voice of `Abdullah bin Qais? Let him come in." `Umar was told that he had left. So, he sent for him and on his arrival, he (Abu Musa) said, "We were ordered to do so (i.e. to leave if not admitted after asking permission thrice). `Umar told him, "Bring witness in proof of your statement." Abu Musa went to the Ansar's meeting places and asked them. They said, "None amongst us will give this witness except the youngest of us, Abu Sa`id Al-Khudri. Abu Musa then took Abu Sa`id Al-Khudri (to `Umar) and `Umar said, surprisingly, "Has this order of Allah's Messenger (ﷺ) been hidden from me?" (Then he added), "I used to be busy trading in markets." [Al-Bukhari, Book 34, Hadith 15]

B- THE SELLING OF THE FOODSTUFF AND ITS STORAGE

حَدَّثَنَا إِسْحَاقُ بْنُ إِبْرَاهِيمَ، أَخْبَرَنَا الْوَلِيدُ بْنُ مُسْلِمٍ، عَنِ الأَوْزَاعِيِّ، عَنِ الزُّهْرِيِّ، عَنْ سَالِمٍ، عَنْ أَبِيهِ ـ رضى الله عنه ـ قَالَ رَأَيْتُ الَّذِينَ يَشْتَرُونَ الطَّعَامَ مُجَازَفَةً يُضْرَبُونَ عَلَى عَهْدِ رَسُولِ اللَّهِ صلى الله عليه وسلم أَنْ يَبِيعُوهُ حَتَّى يُؤْوُوهُ إِلَى رِحَالِهِمْ.

2- Narrated Salim:

that his father said. "I saw those, who used to buy foodstuff without measuring or weighing in the life time of the Prophet (ﷺ) being punished if they sold it before carrying it to their own houses." [Al-Bukhari, Vol. 3, Book 34, Hadith 341/2131]

حَدَّثَنَا مُوسَى بْنُ إِسْمَاعِيلَ، حَدَّثَنَا وُهَيْبٌ، عَنِ ابْنِ طَاوُسٍ، عَنْ أَبِيهِ، عَنِ ابْنِ عَبَّاسٍ ـ رضى الله عنهما ـ أَنَّ رَسُولَ اللَّهِ صلى الله عليه وسلم نَهَى أَنْ يَبِيعَ الرَّجُلُ طَعَامًا حَتَّى يَسْتَوْفِيَهُ. قُلْتُ لاِبْنِ عَبَّاسٍ كَيْفَ ذَاكَ قَالَ ذَاكَ دَرَاهِمُ بِدَرَاهِمَ وَالطَّعَامُ مُرْجَأٌ.

قَالَ أَبُو عَبْدِ اللَّهِ مُرْجَئُونَ مُؤَخَّرُونَ

3- Narrated Tawus:

Ibn `Abbas said, "Allah's Messenger (ﷺ) forbade the selling of foodstuff before its measuring and transferring into one's possession." I asked Ibn `Abbas, "How is that?" Ibn `Abbas replied, "It will be just like selling money for money, as the foodstuff has not been handed over to the first purchaser who is the present seller." [Al-Bukhari, Book 34, Hadith 84]

حَدَّثَنِي أَبُو الْوَلِيدِ، حَدَّثَنَا شُعْبَةُ، حَدَّثَنَا عَبْدُ اللَّهِ بْنُ دِينَارٍ، قَالَ سَمِعْتُ ابْنَ عُمَرَ ـ رضى الله عنهما ـ يَقُولُ قَالَ النَّبِيُّ صلى الله عليه وسلم " مَنِ ابْتَاعَ طَعَامًا فَلاَ يَبِعْهُ حَتَّى يَقْبِضَهُ ".

4-Narrated Ibn `Umar:

The Prophet (ﷺ) said, "He who buys foodstuff should not sell it till he has received it." [Al-Bukhari, Book 34, Hadith 85]

حَدَّثَنَا أَبُو بَكْرِ بْنُ أَبِي شَيْبَةَ، حَدَّثَنَا ابْنُ أَبِي زَائِدَةَ، ح وَحَدَّثَنَا ابْنُ الْمُثَنَّى، حَدَّثَنَا يَحْيَى يَعْنِي ابْنَ سَعِيدٍ، ح وَحَدَّثَنَا ابْنُ نُمَيْرٍ، حَدَّثَنَا أَبِي كُلُّهُمْ، عَنْ عُبَيْدِ اللَّهِ، عَنْ نَافِعٍ، عَنِ ابْنِ عُمَرَ، أَنَّ رَسُولَ اللَّهِ صلى الله عليه وسلم نَهَى أَنْ تُتَلَقَّى السِّلَعُ حَتَّى تَبْلُغَ الأَسْوَاقَ . وَهَذَا لَفْظُ ابْنِ نُمَيْرٍ . وَقَالَ الآخَرَانِ إِنَّ النَّبِيَّ صلى الله عليه وسلم نَهَى عَنِ التَّلَقِّي .

5-Ibn 'Umar (Allah be pleased with them) reported Allah's Messenger (ﷺ) as saying:

Do not go out to meet merchandise in the way, (wait) until it is brought into the market.

This hadith has been reported on the authority of Ibn Numair but with a slight change of words.

[Sahih Muslim, Book 21, Hadith 19]

حَدَّثَنَا ابْنُ أَبِي عُمَرَ، حَدَّثَنَا هِشَامُ بْنُ سُلَيْمَانَ، عَنِ ابْنِ جُرَيْجٍ، أَخْبَرَنِي هِشَامٌ، الْقُرْدُوسِيُّ عَنِ ابْنِ سِيرِينَ، قَالَ سَمِعْتُ أَبَا هُرَيْرَةَ، يَقُولُ إِنَّ رَسُولَ اللَّهِ صلى الله عليه وسلم قَالَ " لاَ تَلَقَّوُا الْجَلَبَ . فَمَنْ تَلَقَّاهُ فَاشْتَرَى مِنْهُ فَإِذَا أَتَى سَيِّدُهُ السُّوقَ فَهُوَ بِالْخِيَارِ" .

6-Abu Huraira (Allah be pleased with him) reported Allah's Messenger (ﷺ) as saying:

<u>Do not meet the merchant</u> in the way and enter into business transaction with him, and whoever meets him and buys from him (and in case it is done, see) that when the owner of (merchandise) comes into the market (and finds that he has been paid less price) he has the option (to declare the transaction null and void). [Sahih Muslim, Book 21, Hadith 23]

C-BUYING THE GOODS AWAY FROM THE MARKET

حَدَّثَنَا مُحَمَّدُ بْنُ بَشَّارٍ، حَدَّثَنَا عَبْدُ الْوَهَّابِ، حَدَّثَنَا عُبَيْدُ اللَّهِ، عَنْ سَعِيدِ بْنِ أَبِي سَعِيدٍ، عَنْ أَبِي هُرَيْرَةَ ـ رضى الله عنه ـ قَالَ نَهَى النَّبِيُّ صلى الله عليه وسلم عَنِ التَّلَقِّي، وَأَنْ يَبِيعَ حَاضِرٌ لِبَادٍ.

7-Narrated Abu Huraira:

The Prophet (ﷺ) <u>forbade the meeting (of caravans) on the way</u> and the selling of goods by an inhabitant of the town on behalf of a desert dweller. [Al-Bukhari, Book 34, Hadith 113]

حَدَّثَنَا مُسَدَّدٌ، حَدَّثَنَا يَزِيدُ بْنُ زُرَيْعٍ، قَالَ حَدَّثَنِي التَّيْمِيُّ، عَنْ أَبِي عُثْمَانَ، عَنْ عَبْدِ اللَّهِ ـ رضى الله عنه ـ قَالَ مَنِ اشْتَرَى مُحَفَّلَةً فَلْيَرُدَّ مَعَهَا صَاعًا. قَالَ وَنَهَى النَّبِيُّ صلى الله عليه وسلم عَنْ تَلَقِّي الْبُيُوعِ.

8-Narrated `Abdullah:

Whoever buys an animal which has been kept un-milked for a long time, could return it, but has to pay a Sa of dates along with it. And the Prophet (ﷺ) <u>forbade meeting the owners of goods</u> on the way away from the market. [Al-Bukhari, Book 34, Hadith 115]

حَدَّثَنَا عَبْدُ اللَّهِ بْنُ يُوسُفَ، أَخْبَرَنَا مَالِكٌ، عَنْ نَافِعٍ، عَنْ عَبْدِ اللَّهِ بْنِ عُمَرَ ـ رضى الله عنهما ـ أَنَّ رَسُولَ اللَّهِ صلى الله عليه وسلم قَالَ ‏ "‏ لاَ يَبِيعُ بَعْضُكُمْ عَلَى بَيْعِ بَعْضٍ، وَلاَ تَلَقَّوُا السِّلَعَ حَتَّى يُهْبَطَ بِهَا إِلَى السُّوقِ ‏"‏‏.‏

9-Narrated `Abdullah bin `Umar:

Allah's Messenger (ﷺ) said, "You should not try to cancel the purchases of one another (to get a benefit thereof), and do <u>not go ahead to meet the caravan</u> (for buying the goods) (but wait) till it reaches the market." [Al-Bukhari, Book 34, Hadith 116]

8 PROMOTION

INTRODUCTION

It is little information about the topic. It might be since the products were scared and normally brought from outside the country. All the available goods were bought when they reached the market. However, perishable products such as butter, milk, and yogurt were sold daily.

It is undesirable to raise voices in the marketplace, which is one of the ways to advertise. The hadith of Abdur Rahman bin `Auf (RA) tells us the people know the markets which were one way of promotion. Thus, the purpose of promotion is to inform the buyer about the market and products available when and where. The aim of the contemporary promotional strategy is to induce the customer to a specific brand because more than one similar product is available. However, there is some product which is in the "production stage" i.e., the production is less than demand; whatever is produced, it is sold. So, there is no need to induce the customer to buy it. However, providing information about product features and availability is part of the promotional strategy.

People in Makkah and elsewhere did inform themselves about the arrival of various caravans and what the caravan was supposed to bring. It implies that the traders were informing people about it though available media. Which was mostly word of mouth. Although the literacy rate was exceptionally low but even than any important matter was put in black and white. One example is the social boycott of Muslims in Makkah; the matter was in writing and was hanged with the wall of Kaaba. It seems permissible to inform about the products and places where they are available but contemporary advertising is far from Islamic concept. (Allah knows better)

PROMOTION: THE DISLIKE OF RAISING VOICES IN THE MARKET

حَدَّثَنَا مُحَمَّدُ بْنُ سِنَانٍ، حَدَّثَنَا فُلَيْحٌ، حَدَّثَنَا هِلاَلٌ، عَنْ عَطَاءِ بْنِ يَسَارٍ، قَالَ لَقِيتُ عَبْدَ اللَّهِ بْنَ عَمْرِو بْنِ الْعَاصِ ـ رضى الله عنهما ـ قُلْتُ أَخْبِرْنِي عَنْ صِفَةِ، رَسُولِ اللهِ صلى الله عليه وسلم فِي التَّوْرَاةِ. قَالَ أَجَلْ، وَاللهِ إِنَّهُ لَمَوْصُوفٌ فِي التَّوْرَاةِ بِبَعْضِ صِفَتِهِ فِي الْقُرْآنِ يَا أَيُّهَا النَّبِيُّ إِنَّا أَرْسَلْنَاكَ شَاهِدًا وَمُبَشِّرًا وَنَذِيرًا، وَحِرْزًا لِلأُمِّيِّينَ، أَنْتَ عَبْدِي وَرَسُولِي سَمَّيْتُكَ الْمُتَوَكِّلَ، لَيْسَ بِفَظٍّ وَلاَ غَلِيظٍ وَلاَ سَخَّابٍ فِي الأَسْوَاقِ، وَلاَ يَدْفَعُ بِالسَّيِّئَةِ السَّيِّئَةَ وَلَكِنْ يَعْفُو وَيَغْفِرُ، وَلَنْ يَقْبِضَهُ اللهُ حَتَّى يُقِيمَ بِهِ الْمِلَّةَ الْعَوْجَاءَ بِأَنْ يَقُولُوا لاَ إِلَهَ إِلاَّ

اللَّهِ. وَيَفْتَحُ بِهَا أَعْيُنًا عُمْيًا، وَآذَانًا صُمًّا، وَقُلُوبًا غُلْفًا. تَابَعَهُ عَبْدُ الْعَزِيزِ بْنُ أَبِي سَلَمَةَ عَنْ هِلَالٍ. وَقَالَ سَعِيدٌ عَنْ هِلَالٍ عَنْ عَطَاءٍ عَنِ ابْنِ سَلَامٍ. غُلْفٌ كُلُّ شَيْءٍ فِي غِلَافٍ، سَيْفٌ أَغْلَفُ، وَقَوْسٌ غَلْفَاءُ، وَرَجُلٌ أَغْلَفُ إِذَا لَمْ يَكُنْ مَخْتُونًا.

1-Narrated Ata bin Yasar:

I met `Abdullah bin `Amr bin Al-`As and asked him, "Tell me about the description of Allah's Messenger (ﷺ) which is mentioned in Torah (i.e. Old Testament.") He replied, 'Yes. By Allah, he is described in Torah with some of the qualities attributed to him in the Qur'an as follows: "O Prophet! We have sent you as a witness (for Allah's True religion) And a giver of glad tidings (to the faithful believers), And a warner (to the unbelievers) And guardian of the illiterates. You are My slave and My messenger (i.e., Apostle). I have named you "Al-Moutawakel" (who depends upon Allah). You are neither discourteous, harsh <u>nor a noisemaker in the markets</u> and you do not do evil to those Who do evil to you, but you deal with them with forgiveness and kindness. Allah will not let him (the Prophet) Die till he makes straight the crooked people by making them say: "None has the right to be worshipped but Allah," With which will be opened blind eyes and deaf ears and enveloped hearts." [Al-Bukhari, Book 34, Hadith 77]

9 VIRTUES OF TRADERS

INTRODUCTION

This small chapter includes several aspects which were not included in any of the topics discussed above.

Two themes are included: virtues of trade/business and the importance of measurement. Ahadith about measurements are also describing the virtues, therefore they are also included under the 'virtues. Six ahadith are included in the chapter.

A-VIRTUES OF TRADERS

حَدَّثَنَا هَنَّادٌ، حَدَّثَنَا قَبِيصَةُ، عَنْ سُفْيَانَ، عَنْ أَبِي حَمْزَةَ، عَنِ الْحَسَنِ، عَنْ أَبِي سَعِيدٍ، عَنِ النَّبِيِّ صلى الله عليه وسلم قَالَ " التَّاجِرُ الصَّدُوقُ الأَمِينُ مَعَ النَّبِيِّينَ وَالصِّدِّيقِينَ وَالشُّهَدَاءِ ". قَالَ أَبُو عِيسَى هَذَا حَدِيثٌ حَسَنٌ لاَ نَعْرِفُهُ إِلاَّ مِنْ هَذَا الْوَجْهِ مِنْ حَدِيثِ الثَّوْرِيِّ عَنْ أَبِي حَمْزَةَ . وَأَبُو حَمْزَةَ اسْمُهُ عَبْدُ اللَّهِ بْنُ جَابِرٍ وَهُوَ شَيْخٌ بَصْرِيٌّ .

1-Abu Sa'eed narrated

that the Prophet (ﷺ) said: "The truthful, trustworthy merchant is with the Prophets, the truthful, and the martyrs." [Abu 'Eisa said:] This Hadith is Hasan, we do not know it except this route, a narration of Ath-Thawri from Abu Hamzah. Abu Hamzah's name is 'Abdullah bin Jabir, and he is a Shaikh from Al-Basrah. [Jami` at-Tirmidhi, Book 14, Hadith 7/1209]

حَدَّثَنَا مُحَمَّدُ بْنُ الصَّبَّاحِ، حَدَّثَنَا إِسْمَاعِيلُ بْنُ زَكَرِيَّاءَ، عَنْ مُحَمَّدِ بْنِ سُوقَةَ، عَنْ نَافِعِ بْنِ جُبَيْرِ بْنِ مُطْعِمٍ، قَالَ حَدَّثَتْنِي عَائِشَةُ ـ رضى الله عنها ـ قَالَتْ قَالَ رَسُولُ اللَّهِ صلى الله عليه وسلم " يَغْزُو جَيْشٌ الْكَعْبَةَ، فَإِذَا كَانُوا بِبَيْدَاءَ مِنَ الأَرْضِ يُخْسَفُ بِأَوَّلِهِمْ وَآخِرِهِمْ ". قَالَتْ قُلْتُ يَا رَسُولَ اللَّهِ كَيْفَ يُخْسَفُ بِأَوَّلِهِمْ وَآخِرِهِمْ، وَفِيهِمْ أَسْوَاقُهُمْ وَمَنْ لَيْسَ مِنْهُمْ. قَالَ " يُخْسَفُ بِأَوَّلِهِمْ وَآخِرِهِمْ، ثُمَّ يُبْعَثُونَ عَلَى نِيَّاتِهِمْ ".

2-Narrated `Aisha:

Allah's Messenger (ﷺ) said, "An army will invade the Ka`ba and when the invaders reach Al-Baida', all the ground will sink and swallow the whole army." I said, "O Allah's Messenger (ﷺ)! How will they sink into the ground while amongst them will be their markets (the people who worked in business and not invaders) and the people not belonging to them?" The Prophet (ﷺ) replied, "all of those people will sink but they will be resurrected and judged according to their intentions." [Al-Bukhari, Book 34, Hadith 71]

حَدَّثَنَا إِبْرَاهِيمُ بْنُ مُوسَى، حَدَّثَنَا الْوَلِيدُ، عَنْ ثَوْرٍ، عَنْ خَالِدِ بْنِ مَعْدَانَ، عَنِ الْمِقْدَامِ بْنِ مَعْدِيكَرِبَ، رضى الله عنه عَنِ النَّبِيِّ صلى الله عليه وسلم قَالَ " كِيلُوا طَعَامَكُمْ يُبَارَكْ لَكُمْ ".

3-Narrated Al-Miqdam bin Ma'diyakrib:

The Prophet (ﷺ) said, "Measure your foodstuff and you will be blessed." [Al-Bukhari, Book 34, Hadith 80]

حَدَّثَنَا عَبْدُ الْعَزِيزِ بْنُ عَبْدِ اللَّهِ، حَدَّثَنَا إِبْرَاهِيمُ بْنُ سَعْدٍ، عَنْ أَبِيهِ، عَنْ جَدِّهِ، قَالَ قَالَ عَبْدُ الرَّحْمَنِ بْنُ عَوْفٍ ـ رضى الله عنه ـ لَمَّا قَدِمْنَا الْمَدِينَةَ آخَى رَسُولُ اللَّهِ صلى الله عليه وسلم بَيْنِي وَبَيْنَ سَعْدِ بْنِ الرَّبِيعِ فَقَالَ سَعْدُ بْنُ الرَّبِيعِ إِنِّي أَكْثَرُ الأَنْصَارِ مَالاً، فَأَقْسِمُ لَكَ نِصْفَ مَالِي، وَانْظُرْ أَىَّ زَوْجَتَىَّ هَوِيتَ نَزَلْتُ لَكَ عَنْهَا، فَإِذَا حَلَّتْ تَزَوَّجْتَهَا. قَالَ فَقَالَ عَبْدُ الرَّحْمَنِ لاَ حَاجَةَ لِي فِي ذَلِكَ، هَلْ مِنْ سُوقٍ فِيهِ تِجَارَةٌ قَالَ سُوقُ قَيْنُقَاعَ. قَالَ فَغَدَا إِلَيْهِ عَبْدُ الرَّحْمَنِ، فَأَتَى بِأَقِطٍ وَسَمْنٍ ـ قَالَ ـ ثُمَّ تَابَعَ الْغُدُوَّ، فَمَا لَبِثَ أَنْ جَاءَ عَبْدُ الرَّحْمَنِ عَلَيْهِ أَثَرُ صُفْرَةٍ، فَقَالَ رَسُولُ اللَّهِ صلى الله عليه وسلم " تَزَوَّجْتَ ". قَالَ نَعَمْ. قَالَ " وَمَنْ ". قَالَ امْرَأَةً مِنَ الأَنْصَارِ. قَالَ " كَمْ سُقْتَ ". قَالَ زِنَةَ نَوَاةٍ مِنْ ذَهَبٍ أَوْ نَوَاةً مِنْ ذَهَبٍ. فَقَالَ لَهُ النَّبِيُّ صلى الله عليه وسلم " أَوْلِمْ وَلَوْ بِشَاةٍ ".

4-Narrated Ibrahim bin Sa`d from his father from his grandfather:

`Abdur Rahman bin `Auf said, "When we came to Medina as emigrants, Allah's Messenger (ﷺ) established a bond of brotherhood between me and Sa`d bin Ar-Rabi`. Sa`d bin Ar-Rabi` said (to me), 'I am the richest among the Ansar, so I will give you half of my wealth and you may look at my two wives and whichever of the two you may choose I will divorce her, and when she has completed the prescribed period (before marriage) you may marry her.' `Abdur-Rahman replied, "I am not in need of all that. Is there any marketplace where trade is practiced?' He replied, "<u>The market of Qainuqa</u>." <u>`Abdur- Rahman went to that market the following day and brought some dried buttermilk (yogurt) and butter, and then he continued going there regularly.</u> A few days later, `Abdur-Rahman came having traces of yellow (scent) on his body. Allah's Messenger (ﷺ) asked him whether he had married. He replied in the affirmative. The Prophet (ﷺ) said, 'Whom have you married?' He replied, 'A woman from the Ansar.' Then the Prophet (ﷺ) asked, 'How much did you pay her?' He replied, '(I gave her) a gold piece equal in weight to a date stone (or a date stone of gold)! The Prophet (ﷺ) said, 'Give a Walima (wedding banquet) even if with one sheep.' " [Al-Bukhari, Book 34, Hadith 2]

5-Cancelling a transaction

وَعَنْ أَبِي هُرَيْرَةَ قَالَ قَالَ رَسُولُ اللَّهِ صَلَّى اللَّهُ عَلَيْهِ وَسَلَّمَ: «مَنْ أَقَالَ مُسْلِمًا أَقَالَه اللَّهُ عَثْرَتَهُ يَوْمَ الْقِيَامَةِ». رَوَاهُ أَبُو دَاوُدَ وَابْنُ مَاجَهْ

وَفِي «شَرْحِ السُّنَّةِ» بِلَفْظِ «الْمَصَابِيحِ» عَنْ شُرَيْحٍ الشَّامِيِّ مُرْسَلا

Abu Huraira reported God's Messenger as saying, "If anyone rescinds a sale with a Muslim, God will cancel his slip (God will forgive his fault.) on the day of resurrection." [Mishkaat al-Masabih 2881; In-book reference: Book 11, Hadith 119]

B-MEASUREMENTS

حَدَّثَنَا إِبْرَاهِيمُ بْنُ مُوسَى، حَدَّثَنَا الْوَلِيدُ، عَنْ ثَوْرٍ، عَنْ خَالِدِ بْنِ مَعْدَانَ، عَنِ الْمِقْدَامِ بْنِ مَعْدِيكَرِبَ، رضى الله عنه عَنِ النَّبِيِّ صلى الله عليه وسلم قَالَ " كِيلُوا طَعَامَكُمْ يُبَارَكْ لَكُمْ ".

6-Narrated Al-Miqdam bin Ma'diyakrib:

The Prophet (ﷺ) said, "Measure your foodstuff and you will be blessed." [Al-Bukhari, Book 34, Hadith 80]

حَدَّثَنَا مُوسَى، حَدَّثَنَا وُهَيْبٌ، حَدَّثَنَا عَمْرُو بْنُ يَحْيَى، عَنْ عَبَّادِ بْنِ تَمِيمٍ الأَنْصَارِيِّ، عَنْ عَبْدِ اللَّهِ بْنِ زَيْدٍ ـ رضى الله عنه ـ عَنِ النَّبِيِّ صلى الله عليه وسلم " أَنَّ إِبْرَاهِيمَ حَرَّمَ مَكَّةَ، وَدَعَا لَهَا، وَحَرَّمْتُ الْمَدِينَةَ كَمَا حَرَّمَ إِبْرَاهِيمُ مَكَّةَ، وَدَعَوْتُ لَهَا فِي مُدِّهَا وَصَاعِهَا، مِثْلَ مَا دَعَا إِبْرَاهِيمُ ـ عَلَيْهِ السَّلاَمُ ـ لِمَكَّةَ ".

7-Narrated `Abdullah bin Zaid:

The Prophet (ﷺ) said, "The Prophet (ﷺ) Abraham made Mecca a sanctuary and asked for Allah's blessing in it. I made Medina a sanctuary as Abraham made Mecca a sanctuary and I asked for Allah's <u>Blessing in its measures the Mudd and the Sa as Abraham did for Mecca</u>. [Al-Bukhari, Book 34, Hadith 81]

حَدَّثَنَا عَبْدُ اللَّهِ بْنُ يُوسُفَ، أَخْبَرَنَا مَالِكٌ، عَنْ نَافِعٍ، عَنْ عَبْدِ اللَّهِ بْنِ عُمَرَ ـ رضى الله عنهما ـ أَنَّ رَسُولَ اللَّهِ صلى الله عليه وسلم قَالَ " مَنِ ابْتَاعَ طَعَامًا فَلاَ يَبِيعُهُ حَتَّى يَسْتَوْفِيَهُ ".

8-Narrated `Abdullah ibn `Umar:

Allah's Messenger (ﷺ) said, "<u>He who buys foodstuff should not sell it till he is satisfied with the measure with which he has bought it</u>." [Al-Bukhari, Book 34, Hadith 78]

حَدَّثَنِي عَبْدُ اللَّهِ بْنُ مَسْلَمَةَ، عَنْ مَالِكٍ، عَنْ إِسْحَاقَ بْنِ عَبْدِ اللَّهِ بْنِ أَبِي طَلْحَةَ، عَنْ أَنَسِ بْنِ مَالِكٍ ـ رضى الله عنه ـ أَنَّ رَسُولَ اللَّهِ صلى الله عليه وسلم قَالَ " اللَّهُمَّ بَارِكْ لَهُمْ فِي مِكْيَالِهِمْ، وَبَارِكْ لَهُمْ فِي صَاعِهِمْ وَمُدِّهِمْ ". يَعْنِي أَهْلَ الْمَدِينَةِ.

9-Narrated Anas bin Malik:

Allah's Messenger (ﷺ) said, "<u>O Allah bestow your

<u>blessings on their measures, bless their Mudd and Sa.</u>" The Prophet (ﷺ) meant the people of Medina. [Al-Bukhari, Book 34, Hadith 82]

10 IMPLICATIONS FOR MANAGERS

GENERAL PRINCIPLES

Working for halal is the best of what a person eats because the prophet (ﷺ) forbade the illegal earning.

However, keeping good relations with relatives is a means of getting *barakah* which requires spending on them through financial help, gifts and inviting them for food. One way of getting halal earnings is to work for someone. For example, the caliph used to receive sustenance allowance from the treasury. It helped them to concentrate on the affairs of Muslims otherwise they had to do something for livelihood.

Islam recommends doing trade in the marketplace where price is known to the buyer, and he has the choice to buy from where he wished.

The concept of halal and haram compels a Muslim to do permissible or impermissible business activities.

Most manufacturing activities produce pollution. It is the social responsibility of manufacturers to reduce it as much as possible. Greenery helps it out; the prophet (ﷺ) forbade the cutting of green grass from the area of the holy land except for one kind of grass which goldsmiths used to use as a raw material. The Prophet exempted cutting trees in war because they are a gift of Allah; they need protection, not destruction.

PRODUCT

Islam emphasizes the legality of products or services. The contemporary marketing theory rarely discusses this aspect. There is no universal understanding of the legality of products. Islam did not allow production, marketing, and distribution of wine in most Muslim countries while is a legal product in non-Muslim areas. Such controversial products also include **slavery**, prostitution, child labor, drugs etc.

The product includes physical artifacts, services, ideas and marketing of personalities. The Prophet prohibited some products such as the sale of dogs, pigs, and their products, alcohol, and making pictures in the Islamic teachings. Men cannot wear silk cloths but they can sell them. Similarly, pictured clothes including cushions (and bed sheets etc.) are not allowed. Also, doubtful products which are neither permissible to use nor allowed to trade.

As far as the services are concerned, the prophet (ﷺ) hired the services of a carpenter and the services of a cupping person (barber).

The skin of a dead animal is permissible. [14] However, the fat of a dead animal should not be sold. [15] Pictures, alcohol, a free man, dead animals, idols, and dog are all illegal to trade. [16-21] Also unborn calves are prohibited. It might be because the baby has not yet been born. He may or may not be born healthy so there is a risk of certainty of the actual product. However, a car or a similar product may be sold because the order has been placed and the product will be manufactured at its turn. The perfection of an animal in the stomach is less likely than a physical artifact. [22] Silver for gold on credit is out of the halal arena. The reason could be the one which is related to 'superior quality and inferior quality' dates as mentioned above.

PROCESS

The prophet (ﷺ) asked businesspeople to be lenient in buying, selling, and demanding back the money. The buyer should get <u>possession</u> of the goods before selling them. Cash and credit transactions are permissible. Al-gharer is a conditional sale which means if a condition would be met then, the buyer will pay or buy. In addition, al-limas is considered as undesirable, i.e., the buyer has the right to examine the product; the more touching is not enough.

Similarly, swearing to build the confidence of potential buyers was not desirable. Also, it is undesirable to deceive or cheat while trading; some unavoidable matters like swearing takes place in business so it was recommended that businesspeople should contribute to worthy causes to offset the negative effects of swearing. Barter falls under the flag of the halal transaction but the exchange of <u>inferior dates</u> for excellent quality is forbidden. It is suggested that inferior products must be sold for money and then superior quality goods should be bought. In contemporary terms, a semi-finished or work-in-process product cannot be exchanged with a finished (ready to use products). It seems like the principle that inferior quality products cannot be exchanged with a superior quality product. Here, there is a chance of cheating for the one who is exchanging inferior quality products. The one who offers superior products can demand whatever he likes for inferior ones. Thus, he can exploit the opponent. The alternative is based upon justice where there is a minimum risk for the parties involved. And there is no compulsion for either party to equate the transaction. In this connection, Mufti Taqi Sahib believes that fruits (dates) on the trees should not be sold for its finished shape (i.e., dry dates) but the same can be sold for money. On the other hand, it is fine to sell/exchange fruits on the tree with wheat. [Tofatul Qari, p. 355]

The seller should show the defects of his products; it saves the rights of the buyer. It also discredits the seller, and his image is damaged. Consequently, repeat purchase will be doubtful.

Silk can be traded but men cannot wear it. ARAYA is allowed [See Inaam Bari, Hadith 2192] Fruits should be sold when they are ready (ripe) for use, but the ARAYA trees are exempted from the rulings. [2189]

TERMS OF TRANSACTIONS

Regarding un-milked animals; it implies that the seller is trying to show that the animal is giving a lot of milk say 2kg because it is left un-milked for a given period of time. The amount of milk is measured (as a mutual understanding) twice or thrice in a day. If it is left un-milked from morning to evening, then it will give more milk in the evening because the milk was accumulated. However, if she was milked regularly with understandable intervals, then less quantity of milk will be obtained. It implies the value of the animal will be less than the one who gives more milk than it.

If any condition against the Islamic law is imposed by either buyer or seller, they shall not hold true (invalid). Therefore, it is not permissible to impose any conditions which do not exist in the sharia.

Unripe fruit is not ready for use either for selling or eating so they should not be traded because there is a <u>risk for the buyer</u>. It implies that unfinished products should not be sold. It applies to any of the parties involved in the trade. They may be spoiled or blighted. If the fruit were spoiled or blights, the owner (not the buyer) would suffer the loss.

The next issue is the trade of pollinated dates. The fruit goes to the seller unless the buyer agrees to own the fruits. It means that if a faulty product is sold then in principle it belongs to the seller unless the buyer accepts the ownership. In some cases, the buyer is happy to accept a faulty product e.g., a property developer buys a broken home to refurbish and resell it.

There is practice in rural areas to sell un-harvested fruits for cash. There is a related issue discussed in ahadith. It is known as al-muzabana which means un-gathered dates should not be sold for dry dates or standing crops for the measured quantity of foodstuff. Similarly, if any matter is not discussed in the ahadith/sharia then a traditional practice can be followed. Town dwellers used to function as a broker to desert dwellers which was forbidden.

There is a time limit for a business transaction; a transaction is valid until the parties separate from each other. However, any agreed conditions can prevail. Preemptive right is given to the joint owner of property, i.e., goods for sale or property for sale.

PRICE

Advanced payment is allowed provided it is paid for a specified weight and for a given period. Abu Bakr (RA) and Umer (RA) used to pay in advance. Price should be estimated just i.e., it should be within the capacity of the one who is buying a product/service. Pledging or security is permissible to buy something on credit. It suggests that deferred payment of price can be protected with security. The purpose is to secure the rights of the seller and force the buyer to pay on time.

PLACE

It is recommended to exchange products in markets because the seller knows the prevalent price of his product. It is easy today but during the times of prophet (ﷺ) people used to bring goods for sale from outside the city, so some buyers approached them outside the city/market and buy stuff cheap. It might or might not be concerned about the market price of the product concerned, therefore, the prophet (ﷺ) asked buyers to buy when the goods reach the marketplace. If the price paid is lower than the market price, the seller has the right to cancel the transaction. In this connection meeting of caravans before it reaches the market is forbidden. It has been seen at the occasion of Eid-u-adha that people bring individual animals from the villages, some people buy of them as soon as they enter the marketplace, which is an accessible area without any limits, i.e., on the roadside of usual shopping centers or area. There are other practices in these transactions. Some people buy animals from the loosely specified markets and take the animals to the car park where buyers park their cars. These people approach them quickly and try to sell them the animals (s) they have bought from inside the market at premium prices. In this case, the buyer does not know what the actual price is or what the business condition inside the market is. It has been seen in Islamabad and Rawalpindi cities of Pakistan. It seems to me the buyers are impeded for approaching the actual market. The ahadith quoted above referred to the seller while the situation referred here is about buyers. However, clarification is needed for such situations. Finally, a buyer needs to take <u>possession</u> of goods before he resells it.

PROMOTION

A single hadith was found about the issue which means to the nearest effect that raising voices in the marketplace were discouraged. However, Islamic teaching does not prevent businesspeople to inform the customer about the availability of various products and their prices.

SHOW FAULT BEFORE SELLING

Yahya related to me from Malik from Yahya ibn Said from Salim ibn Abdullah that Abdullah ibn Umar sold one of his slaves for eight hundred dirhams with the stipulation that he was not responsible for defects. The person who bought the slave complained to Abdullah ibn Umar that the slave had a disease which he had not told him about. They argued and went to Uthman ibn Affan for a decision. The man said, "He sold me a slave with a disease which he did not tell me about." Abdullah said, "I sold him with the stipulation that I was not responsible." Uthman ibn Affan decided that Abdullah ibn Umar should take an oath that he had sold the slave without knowing that he had any disease. Abdullah ibn Umar refused to take the oath, so the slave was returned to him and recovered his health in his possession. Abdullah sold him afterwards for 1500 dirhams.

Malik said, "The generally agreed upon way of doing things among us about a man who buys a female slave and she becomes pregnant, or who buys a slave and then frees him, or if there is any other such matter which has already happened so that he cannot return his purchase, and a clear proof is established that there was a fault in that purchase when it was in the hands of the seller or the fault is admitted by the seller or someone else, is that the slave or slave-girl is assessed for its value with the fault it is found to have had on the day of purchase and the buyer is refunded, from what he paid, the difference between the price of a slave who is sound and a slave with such a defect.

Malik said, "The generally agreed upon way of doing things among us regarding a man who buys a slave and then finds out that the slave has a defect for which he can be returned and meanwhile another defect has happened to the slave whilst in his possession, is that if the defect which occurred to the slave in his possession has harmed him, like loss of a limb, loss of an eye, or something similar, then he has a choice. If he wants, he can have the price of the slave reduced equal with the defect (he bought him with) according to the prices on the day he bought him, or if he likes, he can pay compensation for the defect which the slave has suffered in his possession and return him. The choice is up to him. If the slave dies in his possession, the slave is valued with the defect which he had on the day of his purchase. It is seen what his price would really have been. If the price of the slave on the day of purchase without fault was one hundred dinars, and his price on the day of purchase with fault would have been eighty dinars, the price would be reduced by the difference. These prices are assessed according to the market value on the day the slave was purchased. "

Malik said, "The generally agreed upon way of doing things among us is that if a man returns a slave girl in whom he has found a defect and he has already had intercourse with her, he must pay what he has reduced of her price if she was a virgin. If she was not a virgin, there is nothing against his having had intercourse with her because he had charge of her."

Malik said, "The generally agreed upon way of doing things among us regarding a person, whether he is an inheritor or not, who sells a slave, slave-girl, or animal without a liability agreement is that he is not responsible for any defect in what he sold unless he knew about the fault and concealed it. If he knew that there was a fault and concealed it, his declaration that he was free of responsibility does not absolve him, and what he sold is returned to him."

Malik spoke about a situation where a slave-girl was bartered for two other slave-girls and then one of the slave-girls was found to have a defect in which she could be returned. He said, "The slave-girl worth two other slave- girls is valued for her price. Then the other two slave girls are valued, ignoring the defect which the one of them has. Then the price of the slave-girl sold for two slave-girls is divided between them according to their prices so that the proportion of each of them in her price is arrived at - to the higher priced one according to her higher price, and to the other according to her value. Then one looks at the one with the defect, and the buyer is refunded according to the amount her share is affected by the defect, be it little or great. The price of the two slave-girls is based on their market value on the day that they were bought."

Malik spoke about a man who bought a slave and hired him out on a long-term or short-term basis and then found out that the slave had a defect which needed his return. He said that if the man returned the slave because of the defect, he kept the hire and revenue. "This is the way in which things are done in our city. That is because, had the man bought a slave who then built a house for him, and the value of the house was many times the price of the slave, and he then found that the slave had a defect for which he could be returned, and he was returned, he would not have to make payment for the work the slave had done for him. Similarly, he would keep any revenue from hiring him out because he had charge of him. This is the way of doing things among us."

Malik said, "The way of doing things among us when someone buys several slaves in one lot and then finds that one of them has been stolen, or has a defect, is that he looks at the one he finds has been stolen or the one in which he finds a defect. If he is the pick of those slaves, or the most expensive, or it was for his sake that he bought them, or he is the one in whom people see the most excellence, then the whole sale is returned. If the one who is found to be stolen or to have a defect is not the pick of the slaves, and he did not buy them for his sake, and there is no special virtue which people see in him, the one who is found to have a defect or to have been stolen is returned as he is, and the buyer is refunded his portion of the total price."

VIRTUES OF TRADE

The prophet (ﷺ) bought an animal and gifted it back to its owner. The prophet (ﷺ) engaged in trade with one of his companions and returned the animal as a present to him. Therefore, the companion felt good when he sold his animal (or unwanted product) and was happier when he received the product as a gift. Trade was a popular profession because sahabah, the companions of prophet (ﷺ) used to work as traders. In this connection, it was desirable to sell the goods in some measure or weigh it. It was a blessed action.

Businesspeople are pious people; in the eye of sharia even when they travel with an invading army. Because they did not intend to attack. Their purpose was to go with armed forces for trade rather than capturing land and snatching possessions of the people. Allah (SWT) will save from bad resurrection in the Hereafter.

Table 1 Details of Ahadith included in each chapter	
Chapter	Number of ahadith
2	14
3	16
4	33
5	18
6	6
7	9
8	1
9	6
Total	103

BIBLIOGRAPHY

An-Nawawi, Imam Abu Zakaria Mohiuddin Yahya (RA): Translation by Ustadha Aisha, Bewley, http://www.central-mosque.com.

An-Nawawi, Imam Abu Zakaria Mohiuddin Yahya (RA) Abridged edition, New Jersey: Tughra Books.

Iqbal Javed and Muhammad Mushtaq Ahmad (2009) Planning in the Islamic Tradition: The Case of Hijrah Expedition, INSIGHT, Vol.1, No. 3, pp. 37-68.

Kandhelvi, Muhammad Yusuf (NA) Muntakhab Ahadith, Maktaba Faiz Aam, New Dehli.

Muhammad ibn Isma`il al-Bukhari al-Ju`fi (1983) Sahih Al-Bukhari, Translated by Muhammad Muhsin Khan (Translator) Lahore: Kazi Publications.

Muslim ibn al-Ḥajjāj al-Qushayrī (1971-75) Translated by Abdul Hameed Siddiqui Sahih Muslim, Lahore, Sh. Muhammad Ashraf.

Palanpuri, Saeed Ahmad and Hussain Ahmad (2012) Tofatul-Qari, V. 5, Maktabah Hijaaz: Deoband (UP), India.

Abu-AlHasan, Muhammad (2009) Faizul Bari (Urdu Translation of Fatal Bari of Ibn-e-Hajar Alasqalani), V. 3, Maktabah Ashabul Hadith, New Urdu Bazar: Lahore.

Usmani, Muhammad Taqi (2009) Inamulbari, V. 3, Maktabah Al_Alhara: Karachi.

Zakariya, Molana (1979) Faza'il-e-Tijaarat, Idara Ishaat-e-Diniyat (P) Ltd: Dehli.

INDEX

Abi Dawud 18, 19
Al-Bukhari 13, 14, 15, 16, 17, 19, 20, 23, 24, 25, 26, 27, 28, 29, 30, 31, 32, 33, 37, 38, 39, 40, 41, 42, 43, 44, 45, 46, 47, 48, 49, 50, 51, 52, 53, 54, 55, 56, 61, 62, 64, 65, 66, 67, 69, 70, 71, 74, 75, 76, 77, 82, 83, 84, 85, 86, 90, 93, 95, 96
Al-Bukhari, Book 34, Hadith 121 44
Al-Bukhari, Book 34, Hadith 150 66
Alcohol 26, 27, 28, 99
Allah xii, xiv, xvi, 13, 14, 15, 16, 17, 18, 19, 23, 24, 25, 26, 27, 28, 29, 30, 31, 32, 33, 37, 38, 40, 41, 42, 43, 44, 46, 47, 48, 49, 50, 51, 54, 56, 61, 62, 63, 64, 65, 66, 67, 68, 69, 70, 71, 74, 75, 82, 83, 84, 85, 86, 89, 92, 94, 95, 96
Allah's Messenger 13, 14, 15, 16, 17, 19, 23, 24, 25, 26, 27, 28, 29, 30, 31, 32, 37, 40, 41, 43, 44, 46, 47, 48, 49, 50, 51, 54, 56, 61, 62, 63, 64, 65, 66, 67, 68, 70, 71, 74, 75, 82, 83, 84, 85, 86, 89, 92, 94, 96
Animal 16, 25, 86, 102
Araya 49, 50, 54, 55, 56
Blights 65, 103
Broker 69
Business Transaction 17, 85

Butter 94
Buyer xv, 1, 5, 40, 41, 52, 64, 65, 66, 69, 70, 102, 103
Camel 15, 31, 40, 41
Caravan 6, 16, 86
Condition 4, 40, 62, 102
Conditions 5, 62
Dates 3, 16, 24, 43, 44, 46, 50, 51, 54, 55, 56, 61, 63, 65, 67, 74, 75, 86
Day Of Resurrection 28, 31
Desert Dweller 16, 69, 85
Dinar 17, 47, 55
Doubtful Products 99
Earnings 13, 29, 30, 97
Foodstuff 39, 67, 77, 82, 83, 84, 93, 95, 96
Forgiveness 89
Gold 31, 32, 40, 43, 45, 46, 47, 49, 94, 116
Grapes 44, 67, 75
Hadith 13, 14, 15, 16, 17, 18, 19, 20, 24, 25, 26, 27, 28, 29, 30, 31, 32, 33, 37, 38, 39, 40, 41, 42, 43, 44, 45, 46, 47, 48, 49, 50, 51, 52, 53, 54, 55, 56, 61, 62, 64, 65, 66, 67, 69, 70, 71, 74, 75, 76, 77, 82, 83, 84, 85, 86, 90, 93, 95, 96
Hazrat Abdur Rehman Bin Ouff's (RA) 6
Idhkhir 20

Illegal Earning 97	Price 4, 5, 29
Inferior 3, 52	Price Of A Dog 29, 30
Inferior Quality 3, 52	Product Xvi, 1, 2, 3, 4, 5, 38, 41, 98
Iqra 116	Production 98
Jews 26, 29	Promotion .... Xv, 2, 6
Khaibar 51	Prophet 1, 5, 6, 97, 98, 100
Laborer 28	Prophet 13, 14, 15, 16, 18, 19, 20,
Manumitted 39, 76	24, 25, 27, 28, 31, 32, 33, 37, 38,
Market Xvi, 5, 6, 16, 17, 39, 42, 69,	39, 42, 44, 45, 48, 49, 51, 52, 53,
84, 85, 86, 88, 94	55, 56, 62, 68, 69, 70, 74, 75, 76,
Marketing ...... Xv, 1, 2, 5, 98, 116	77, 83, 84, 85, 86, 89, 93, 94, 95,
Measured 54, 67, 102	96
Mecca 19, 28, 95	Riba 30, 43, 44, 45, 46, 48, 51
Medina 56, 74, 75, 94, 95, 96	Ripe 45, 50, 55, 64, 65
Merchandise 84, 85	Sa 16, 18, 23, 24, 26, 41, 47, 50, 51,
Mixed Dates 50, 51, 52	55, 61, 82, 86, 94, 95, 96
Mosque 23	Sahih Muslim 17, 84, 85
Mosque 27	Seller Xv, 5, 6, 45, 52, 63, 64, 66,
Mudd 95, 96	69, 70, 83, 102
Narrated 12, 13, 14, 15, 16, 17,	Services .... Xiv, Xv, 1, 3, 5, 98, 99
18, 19, 23, 24, 25, 26, 27, 28, 29,	Sheep 25, 33, 61, 95
30, 31, 32, 33, 37, 38, 39, 40, 41,	Silk 99
42, 43, 44, 45, 46, 47, 48, 49, 50,	Silver 31, 32, 40, 46, 47, 49
51, 52, 53, 54, 55, 56, 61, 62, 64,	Sink 92
65, 66, 67, 68, 69, 70, 71, 74, 75,	Slave-Girl 30, 62
76, 77, 82, 83, 84, 85, 86, 89, 92,	Swearing 18
93, 94, 95, 96	Tattoos 30
Pay In Advance 74, 75	Torah 89
Payment 5, 31, 48, 75, 77	Transaction 4, 17, 85
Pictures 26, 30, 99	Un-Milked 16, 61, 86, 102
Place 5	Wages 28
Pollinated Date-Palms 66	Weighing 83
Possession 83	Yogurt 94
Price Xv, 1, 2, 4, 5, 28, 29, 30, 31,	Zakariya 1
39, 40, 41, 69, 74, 76, 85	

ABOUT THE AUTHOR

Dr. Javed Iqbal was born on 16 April 1959 in Rawalakot district Poonch Azad Kashmir. He received his early education from Pilot High School Rawalakot and received his matriculation in 1975 and intermediate from Hussain Shaheed Degree College of the same town. He earned a BBA with a gold medal and an MBA with a gold medal from Azad Jammu and Kashmir University in 1986. He was appointed as a lecturer in Business Administration at the same university. Later, he was selected by the government of Pakistan for higher studies and deputed to the United Kingdom. He received an MBA from the University of Hull and Ph.D. from the University of Salford. Dr. Iqbal has been working in England in various roles: professor, director of studies, marketing advisor and academic advisor. Dr. Iqbal returned to Home in 2006 and joined Iqra

University Islamabad campus as an associate professor. He became the head of the department of technology Management in International Islamic University Islamabad (IIUI). He went back to England for some time and rejoined IIUI in 2012. He joined AKU (AJ&K) as professor and Dean Faculty of Management Sciences in March 2015.

He is a distinguished teacher and world-famous scholar. His article title "Learning from a Doctoral Research Project: Structure and Content of a Research Proposal" has been classed by one of the professors as the best piece of knowledge for doctoral students at Deakin University in Australia. This paper is widely used and referred all over the world. Dr. Javed Iqbal has been nominated by an international organization for the Award of Distinguished Scientist for his research contribution this year. His books on various subjects are available on www.amazon.com.

OTHER BOOKS BY THE AUTHOR (S)

1. Iqbal, Javed Saani (2016) Muhammad: His Trials and Tribulations, available on amazon.co.uk. (Paperback edition)
2. Iqbal, Javed Saani (2016) Research Proposals: Contents & Exemplars, available on amazon.co.uk. (Paperback edition)
3. Iqbal, Javed Saani (2016) Responsibilities of Managers: Selected Ahadith, available on amazon.co.uk. (Paperback edition)
4. Iqbal, Javed Saani (2016) Experience: The Journey of My Life, available on amazon.co.uk. (Paperback edition)
5. Iqbal, Javed Saani (2015) Managing Projects, available on amazon.co.uk. (Paperback edition)
6. Iqbal, Javed Saani Understanding Information Systems (2012), Manchester: GRaASS.
7. 6. Iqbal, Javed Saani (2011) Information Systems for Managers, Manchester: GRaASS.
8. Iqbal, Javed Saani, (2011) Digital Divide in South Asia (Paperback edition)
9. Iqbal, Javed Saani, and Muhammad Rafi Khattak Managing Risk in Projects (2011) (Paperback

edition)
10. Iqbal, Javed Saani, and Muhammad Nadeem Understanding Project Management (2011) (Paperback edition)

NOTES

www.ingramcontent.com/pod-product-compliance
Lightning Source LLC
Chambersburg PA
CBHW061439180526
45170CB00004B/1474